Sci.fi & fantasy modeller presents

REAL SPACE
MODELLER

VOLUME ONE

Contents

Sci.fi & fantasy modeller presents

REAL SPACE MODELLER

VOLUME ONE

Copyright © Happy Medium Press 2009

Published by Happy Medium Press
ISBN: 978-0-9558781-7-6

Printed in the United Kingdom by Pioneer Print Solutions.

web: www.scififantasymodeller.co.uk
editorial email: info@scififantasymodeller.co.uk

Contributors: Mike Adamson, Pete Malaguti, Alun Owen, Andy Pearson, Paul Taglianetti, B. P. Taylor, Mike Tucker, Gary R. Welsh.

Editor/co-Publisher: Michael G. Reccia.
Art Editor/co-Publisher: David Openshaw.

Re-released in limited numbers in early 2009 but sadly already a memory (unless you happen to find a dealer who still holds stocks) are *Aoshima's* large-scale *Lunar Module Eagle-5*, together with the company's 1/96 *Apollo – Command Module + Lunar Module, Apollo Saturn V and Lunar Module* and *Apollo Saturn and Landing Ship* plated.

Revell have re-released five of their Real Space subjects into the UK market – their gigantic 1:96 scale *Apollo: Saturn V* kit (see articles elsewhere in this Volume); a 1:96 scale *Apollo: Columbia and Eagle*; a 1/48 scale *Apollo: Lunar Module Eagle*; 1/32nd *Apollo: Spacecraft and Interior* and, finally, a 1/8th *Apollo: Astronaut on The Moon* kit. Each box comes with paints and glue and is badged with a 'Forty Years' roundel.

From *Tamiya* comes a reissue of their 1:100 *Space Shuttle Orbiter*, featuring cockpit interior with decals and figures, 'space lab' cargo, mirrored cargo bay door interiors, rudder with airbrake feature and instruction sheets in Japanese and English with photographs of key components.

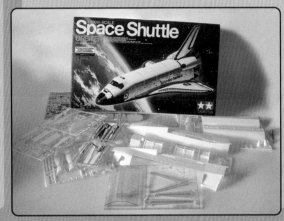

Mission: re-release!
A look at some of the Real Space kits available in this Moon Landing Anniversary year.

Airfix have re-issued their classic *Saturn V* 1:144 scale kit with modified tooling, a new stand, and an accurised top section. *One Small Step For Man* is a re-release of their 1:72 *Lunar Module* in a gift set which includes paints, glue and brushes, a set of 16 *Apollo* Astronauts and a new vac-formed base.

Most of the subjects listed here will be featured as comprehensive build articles in future issues of either **Real Space Modeller** or sister publication **Sci.fi & Fantasy Modeller** (www.scififantasymodeller.co.uk).

Special thanks to *Revell* and to HobbyLink Japan (www.hlj.com) for review kits.

Big thanks, too, to Des and Modelzone Manchester for their help in preparing this feature.

The Next Step

Building Revell's Space Shuttle and Boosters

Article and photographs by **Andy Pearson**

As I spend much of my time building and writing about science fiction and fantasy kit subjects, the chance of constructing some real space hardware for this title was a rare treat. It also provided an opportunity for a little nostalgia as, half a lifetime ago, I had been lucky enough to visit the *Kennedy Space Centre*. This was shortly after the *Apollo* missions had come to an end and plans were afoot for the next stage in space exploration: the *shuttle*.

Whilst I had a great fondness for the *Apollo* programme, there was something about the proposed *shuttle* missions that I found even more attractive as they would involve spacecraft that would be capable of making the 'round trip', as it were. At this point I must confess to experiencing a degree of disappointment when the real thing was unveiled. You see, I had been brought up on a diet of science fiction in books, films and comics, all of which featured spacecraft that were sleek, sensational and fabulous. I had also, thanks to a slightly eccentric and rather reclusive uncle, been exposed to articles in *National Geographic* and similar publications detailing developments of the early experimental lifting bodies such as the *Northrop HL-10* and the *Dyna-Soar* space gliders, which looked fantastic to my young and eager eyes. As a result of all that anticipation my initial reaction to the *shuttle* itself was, '*Is that it?*'

Once I became familiar with the new ship on the block, however, my initial disappointment quickly melted away, which I'm sure came as a blessed relief to *NASA* and all involved in the project.

The *Revell* kit I was given for this review was a conventional injection moulded model to 1:144 scale, which would build into the *shuttle* itself, the two solid fuel boosters, the external fuel tank and a transport and launch platform. This latter component really

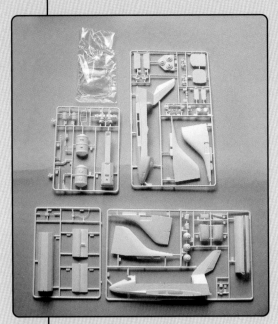

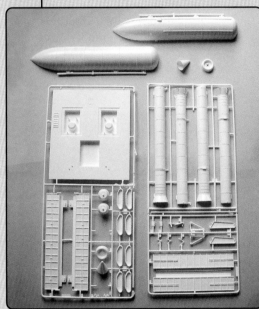

got the nostalgia juices flowing as I have actually stood alongside one of the crawler units on this beast and, somewhere, there's a photograph to prove it. I believe that the same basic mobile launch platform that was used for the *Saturn 5* rocket is still used for *shuttle* launches.

I have rarely been furnished with such an array of reference materials before starting a model. In this case, three wonderful books on the history and development of the *shuttle* were provided by Steve Davies, a model maker of some renown and a fellow contributor to sister title *Sci.fi & Fantasy Modeller*. It really was a pleasure to have all the required information to hand rather than having to scamper around the Internet, particularly as my pathetic broadband connection doesn't really do scampering, even on a good day, but that's one of the joys of living in the sticks.

Step one was to bring the two halves of the *shuttle's* fuselage together, including a rear bulkhead and the moveable baffle that sits below the engine bells. Step two was to ponder the best way of making up the discrepancy in depth between the right and left cockpit window apertures, which was, in model terms, considerable. I considered using filler such as *Milliput* or *Squadron White Stuff* but the area that needed building up was so small that even the best fillers would be too brittle for comfort. The eventual solution was to laminate several layers of thin plastic card together to make up the required depth and then cut a thin shape from these to follow the upper contour of the cockpit aperture. This was a somewhat delicate operation as the actual transparency supplied with the kit serves not only the main windscreen but also the two view ports above the forward cabin, meaning the plastic card insert had to follow these complex lines. An hour of so of fiddling and the job was done.

Having had that one early experience with less than perfect fit it seemed logical to leap ahead in the recommended build sequence and assemble any other parts that looked as though they might require further preparation or filling. I'd also decided to prime the model, which is something I rarely do with injection moulded kits, so as many components as possible in place before that step would help. The kit comes with a fairly detailed cargo bay and working bay doors so that the *shuttle* can be displayed with its doors open, to show the interior and cargo, or with them closed. Truth to tell the cargo was still quite visible with the doors closed due to gaps. That fact led to the decision to seal the doors permanently and fill said gaps, which was not really a problem as I'd opted to display the model in its launch position anyway.

In order to fit the cargo bay doors correctly it was necessary to include a forward bulkhead behind the crew cabin and, in my haste to proceed, I made my first error by failing to allow for the final appearance of the cabin interior through the windscreen and

Shuttle and cargo components from the box.

Fuel tank, solid fuel rocket boosters and crawler parts.

view ports. On reflection, the interior would have been better painted overall in a dark grey as, on the final model, it is fairly obviously empty. There is, of course, the prospect of scratch-building an interior upper deck but time really didn't permit such an indulgence.

As it transpired, two or three days were needed to fill around the cargo bay doors using several very thin beads of *Milliput*, allowing for drying times and the delicate procedure of scribing the lines at the bay door extremities. Then came the wings, with more filling round the wing roots and another of those valuable lessons gained through hindsight. Handling the fuselage to fit and fill the wings resulted in hairline cracks appearing around the completed bay doors and, in one or two places, the loss of complete sections of filler. I decided to ignore this problem until the wings were fixed to my satisfaction and this was a relatively easy task. I again used the fine white grade of *Milliput* here and a technique for smoothing same, which I've described in detail in previous issues of *SF&FM*. If you'll indulge me in a little repetition this involves using silicon rubber-tipped modelling tools, moistened with water and run along the seams that have been filled before the filler is fully set.

With the wings firmly and cleanly in place my attention turned to repairing the filler round the bay doors. Should you choose to build this kit I would recommend bracing and strengthening the bay doors and the *shuttle*'s fuselage as much as possible internally if you intend to display them closed. This will help avoid cracks appearing due to the flexibility of the plastic itself.

With the main components in place and the transparencies at the front masked I gave the whole model several coats of white car primer and allowed twenty-four hours for this to dry. If I had been using the excellent references referred to earlier alone I would have then painted the kit with a gloss white, the better to fix the decals, and topped this with a semi-matt coat of clear acrylic. According to the instructions, however, the overall colour is a mixture of 50% light grey silky matt and 50% white silky matt, and a good match for this is found in the decals supplied for the rudder and the trailing edges of the wings. In truth, the real thing still looks white to me but I suspect that the hint of grey is intended to simulate to some extent the vast amount of surface texture that's a feature of the *shuttle*. Shall I confess to a mistake at this point? They say that confession is good for the soul, both within and without the religious context, but I'll get my excuses in first. Having mixed the white and grey paint as suggested I decided to experiment with the actual finish using the conical ends of the two solid fuel boosters as my test pieces. These I airbrushed with slightly differing mixtures of the colour and set them aside to dry, at which point the editorial team had a change of mind as to the priority of the models I was building for the regular editions of *Sci.fi & Fantasy Modeller*. As a result the *shuttle* kit was set aside for a few weeks whilst

Top: building up the shortfall in the cockpit aperture with plastic card.

Above: paint added to wings.

Below: the *shuttle*'s cargo…

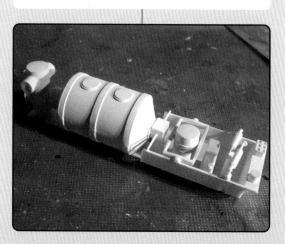

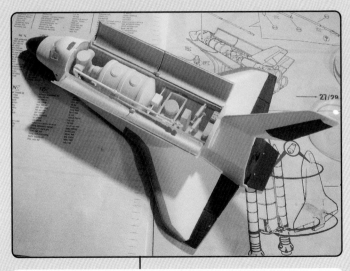

Above: ...and cargo installed in the cargo bay.

Below: spot the gap!

Bottom: the gaps between cargo bay doors and fuselage are filled.

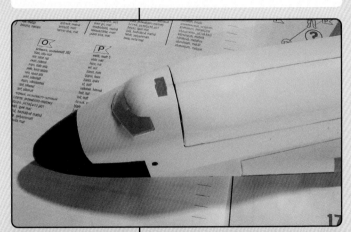

I worked on other subjects and it was only after the two boosters had been built, painted, had their multitude of decals applied and had been sealed with a clear acrylic that I realised that the nose cone of each booster was a slightly different shade. I intend to amend this situation but in the interim will be telling people that it's a trick of the light, so keep the above to yourself if you will.

Back to the *shuttle*. There are significant areas that require further painting, with greys to the leading edges of the wings, anthracite to the under parts of the craft and selected panels needing to be semi-gloss black. The painting directions provided for these areas are very comprehensive but involve measurements in millimetres and some angles that have to be lifted from the instruction sheet and transferred to the model. Attention to detail was obviously going to be vital but some saving grace was provided by the decals, several of which actually form an edging to the semi-gloss back areas round the *shuttle*'s nose. This was particularly useful at the very tip of the craft's nose, which is a roundel of blue-grey. Here a decal gives a nice, sharp edge to this area and, indeed, seems to have been included for this very purpose.

Two long and very narrow decals run either side of the loading bay doors and provide the details of what I assume to be hinges. These, somewhat to my surprise, went on in one piece quite easily and that prompts me to comment on the quality of the decals overall, which is excellent. There were also two decals which ran along the leading edges of the wings, providing a demarcation line between the grey forward edge of the wing and the off-white of the main *shuttle* colour. These certainly benefited from being cut in half and fitted as two pieces and there was a very obvious place to separate them. When positioning the first of these it became obvious that there wasn't going to be a fit between the decal and the lower anthracite-painted portion of the fuselage, leaving a sliver of the off-white between the two. This, I thought, could be tricky, as it would possibly require some masking and, in my experience, masking tape and decals, even decals oversprayed with clear acrylic, can be a recipe for disaster. I then had one of my rare flashes of inspiration, of which I'm allowed one or two a year. Within the spares box lurked some black stripe *Xtradecals* which allowed me to cover the gaps perfectly and which, by way of a bonus, provided some almost invisible extra texture to the area, of which the real *shuttle* has a lot, thanks to the multitude of heat-resisting tiles that cover large portions of its surface.

This is probably a good place to pause and point out that the decals and options for the *shuttle* give modellers the choice of eight of the orbiters: *Enterprise*, *Discovery*, *Atlantis* and *Endeavour* in pre and post 1998 versions. I was, incidentally, building the pre-1998 *Endeavour*.

Meanwhile, back at the model, 'twas time to seal the decals in place with an overall coat of semi-matt clear acrylic, but what I didn't want was semi-matt windows or view ports. I've just touched on the hazards of making tape and decals and, despite having given the area around the transparencies a precautionary coat of clear gloss acrylic, I was keen to find a low tack masking agent. Now damp newsprint can work quite well but there's always the possibility of the pressure of the airbrush spray blowing it off the model and here I was dealing with eight separate and very small clear components. In the event I used small sections of the adhesive strips from *Post-it* notes, which are, by their very nature, sticky, but not very.

The model was, incidentally, provided with the option of the undercarriage in the landing position and the *shuttle*'s three main engines can be positioned to simulate the gimballing of the real thing.

The construction of the two solid fuel boosters and the external tank was very straightforward. All three required a little filling along the seams with *Squadron White Stuff*, priming and painting with the same colour as the *shuttle* itself in the case of the boosters. As with the *shuttle*, decals provided the options of early and later versions of the boosters and there were also options identified for panels in the launch position or start position, although I'm somewhat at a loss to understand why these panels should change once the engines have fired. Other than the nose cones, the only additional components on the boosters were the engine bells and the smaller engines which, I

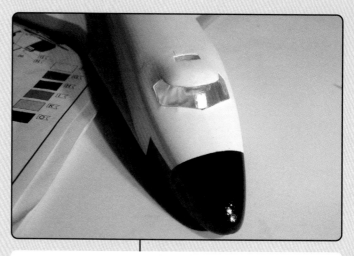

Above: the restored windscreen aperture with the transparent component in place.

Below: masking for the nose area.

Bottom: rear view of shuttle showing engine detail and control surfaces.

Above: decals in place on finished *shuttle*.

Below: adding some detail to the crawler unit tracks.

Bottom: colour scheme on external fuel tank applied.

assume, fire the boosters away from the *shuttle* after their fuel is exhausted so that they can parachute back to Earth for recovery and re-use.

The external fuel tank is interesting, although the build entailed little more than bringing the two halves together and filling seams. The fascinating aspect was the subtlety of the colour, a good guide to which was provided with the instructions. I followed this as the colour of the tank in the many references I had for it varied from almost orange to a buff-brown, depending on the light conditions. The tank colour is, apparently, that of the insulation used on its surface and it's perhaps worth noting that, in the very earliest launches, the tanks were painted white until this was deemed unnecessary, the paint's removal for subsequent launches also saving around 600 lbs in weight that could be used for additional payload. There are three slightly varying shades of a light brown on the tank itself.

The launch platform was also a very basic construction and does not include all the detail to be found on the real thing. There was plenty of opportunity to scratchbuild some additional components and features but, with a brief to build from the box and some time constraints, the only changes I made were to the four crawler units. These lacked a certain amount of detail, particularly in the area of the caterpillar tracks, which only had moulding on the external track surface. The work of an hour or so with some careful measuring and a scriber soon amended that. The track units were then given an overall wash of thinned black ink to pick out some of the detail. The launch platform is probably the only area of the model in its launch configuration where some weathering could be justified and this was attended to with various shades of mid and dark grey washes and airbrush coats.

This is, I suspect, a re-issued kit, the copyright date on the instructions for the version I had being 2006, and it assembles into a satisfying model for fans of real space travel. There are also lots of opportunities for customising for hyper-realism, as there's a lot of texture on the *shuttle* that isn't presented in the moulding on the kit. Simulating this and including features such as the cockpit interior would be time consuming but, I imagine, very rewarding, so much so that I'm inclined to buy another kit and do just that at some time in the future.

On a final note there are, I'm sure, future generations and designs of *shuttles* to come, and there are also many fascinating prospective kits to be based on craft that featured in the experimental stages that resulted in the *shuttle*'s creation. One I'd love to see is the proposal put forward by German industrial designer Luigi Colani for a single-stage *shuttle* capable of carrying all its propellant on board. See if you can track any images of it down next time you're on the Internet. Now *that's* a spaceship.

Above: solid fuel rocket boosters.

Left: a bird's eye view of finished model.

Opposite page: completed model atop its crawler.

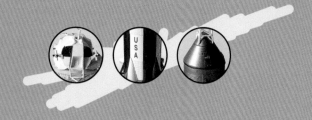

Saturn V three-stage modelling mission — Stage One:
From the box
1994 Revell
1/96 release
Article and photographs by Andy Pearson

This is a big kit of a big booster in an even bigger box, for which the marketing people at *Revell* deserve a tip of the hat because, as a sales strategy, the packaging is a master stroke. The fact of the matter is that the contents would fit in a container a third of the size of the one this kit comes in, but imagine the impact on the young and eager modeller of the huge pack. 'This,' they would think, 'is going to be a big, *big* kit.' And it is – the completed model standing around four feet tall. *Revell*'s perennial 1:96 *Saturn V* kit, initially released in 1970, has been re-issued several times. In 1982 it was re-released as a *History Makers* subject and, in 1994, as a *Selected Subjects* model, which is the version I'll be building for this article.

Like many *Revell* kits of the period, the *Saturn V* is something of a curate's egg in as much as parts of it are excellent. On the other hand I don't think I've ever encountered a model that has been the subject of so many negative Web reviews... not, it must be stressed, so much about the quality but more concerning the accuracy. Before I began the build I indulged in a Net search for as much reference material as I could gather and the very first website I came across was unflattering. A subsequent chat with a fellow modeller who is something of an authority on rocketry in fact and fiction revealed that he, too, was less than enthusiastic about the kit under discussion, again from the viewpoint of authenticity.

In terms of the building of the rocket I found nothing to place great demands on the patience of the moderately experienced modeller but there *were* some oddities and frustrations. The first bit of strangeness was the fact that most of the larger cylindrical sections are supplied as flat sheets of plastic card printed (silk screened, if my print technology insights haven't deserted me entirely) with the various markings and insignia. These need to be formed into cylinders and are then held in position by injection-moulded sections sitting on the outer and inner surfaces and located through pre-punched holes. It occurred to me here that, although

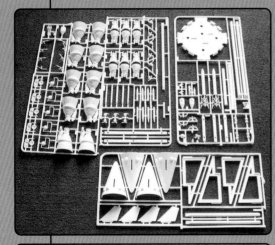

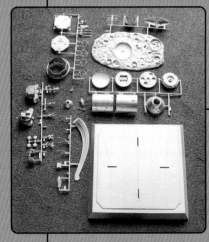

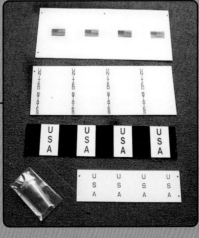

the rod that would receive the adhesive would be hidden within the cylindrical section, an excess of liquid poly could do all sorts of nasty things to the thin plastic card. This being the case I decided to use superglue on all these sections to avoid any mishaps. It's probably also worth pointing out that it is very easy to accidentally crease these cylindrical parts when handling them.

The first step was to build the base on which the model would rest and this is a simple, square platform with four supports. Next came the mighty first stage engines, of which there are five. Each engine bell is supplied in two halves and benefits from quite a lot of smoothing and filling to hide the joins. A further four components are added for each engine, the assembly of which is quite straightforward. The engines then locate into a base plate, which, in turn, fits into an injection moulded sleeve that forms the lower section of the first stage and accepts the first of the plastic card cylinders. This lower section also carries four, half-cone shaped outer housings for the engines plus four fins which locate onto these.

Much of my initial desk research concerned the paint scheme for the model and there does seem to be quite a lot of variance in this depending on which generation of *Saturn V* one is looking at. Having said that, this first stage seems to be common to all and the painting only required the matching of the vertical black bands on the lower collar with those on the printed card insert. Similarly, the conical housings and fins needed to match up but a degree of test fitting revealed that, once in place, these didn't bisect the main black bands exactly in the centre as they should have done. This resulted in a little juggling and, to be honest, some compromise.

The next stage comprised of one of the cylinders formed from the pre-printed plastic card topped with another injection moulded collar that leads to the stage two assemblies. The collar also features the vertical black bands and these obviously needed to match the bands at the base of this stage. Achieving this required what would become something of a ritual: the counting of ribs. You see, most of the intermediate collars feature a vertical ribbing and it was, in fact, this that seemed to draw most of the opprobrium from the harsher critics of the kit on the basis that some of it shouldn't be there at all. Some of the better

Previous page: the completed *Saturn V* showing *Lunar Module* with landing legs deployed.

This page: the various components of *Revell*'s 1:96 scale *Saturn V* kit. Note the final photograph showing the flat, screen-printed sheets that make up the cylindrical sections of the rocket's three stages.

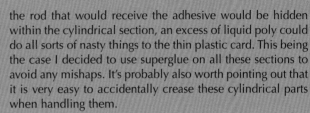

references I found were supplied by a friend who had photographed the real thing during a visit to Florida and, whilst his collection of images wasn't exhaustive, the ribs did seem to be present on all the relevant shots he supplied. Ribbed areas and their exact locations and dimensions are probably a subject best left to the experts. The advantage of the ribs from a modelling point of view is that they provide a relatively easy way of matching the vertical banding stage by stage, although they don't always line up exactly... to expect them to do so would probably be a criticism too far for a kit of this type and vintage.

The uppermost collars of both stages one and two also require a horizontal banding and this was where the ribbing presented some minor problems. No matter how carefully masking tape was applied it proved almost impossible to get it to fit perfectly into the 'valleys' between the ribs, even when using double or triple layers of tape and techniques such as easing lengths into place one rib at a time using the back of a scalpel blade. As a result, even with a fairly low pressure on the airbrush some of the sprayed paint crept under the tape. The only solution seemed to be to live with this and scrape away any excess with a blade once the paint was dry. This was a somewhat tedious operation but not exhaustingly so.

Following the completion of the two collars between stages one and two came the assembly of the stage two engines but this needs to be preceded by a confession. The main separation collar features eight small external engines (I assume that's what they are) which, presumably, were designed to aid the separation of the stages. When referring to the instructions again in the process of writing this piece I discovered that they are designated as being 'dust grey' in colour – and I've rendered them as either black or white to match the surface on which they're located. *Whoops!*

The stage two engines are again a straightforward assembly of just four components apiece and, in fact, the stage three engine is the same size and configuration as these, so it was also assembled at this juncture. The plastic card provided to create the main component of stage two proved not to be perfectly square and risked giving the model a slight lean, so some careful trimming was required. At the top of the second stage are two further collars, the uppermost of these tapering to stage three, The painting of this tapering component was even more 'fun' than the previous ones as the ribbing also tapered and the 'valleys' were narrower, meaning more scraping was necessary.

Top: the completed first stage engine section.
Centre: Stage one in progress – the flat sheet is formed into a cylinder and held in place by injection pieces that slot through pre-punched holes.
Bottom: Stage one nears completion.

The third stage assembly follows the same procedures described above except that this is the stage that would accommodate the *LEM* or *Lunar Excursion Module...* or would it? The *Module* itself could be assembled in its stowed position with the landing legs folded or it could be displayed with deployed legs (along with an astronaut figure, the *Command Module* and the *Service Module*) on and above a not very convincing moon base. Would you indulge me in a brief 'when I was a lad' moment? When I was a lad – well, in my very early twenties – the moon landings were still events of great international excitement and the model makers obviously produced kits to celebrate this fact. I built a model of the *LEM* and created a lunar landscape for this to sit in. It was obvious from the images coming from the landings that the moon's surface wasn't quite the towering crater rims and spiked peaks that SF illustrators had so lovingly rendered, so I went for something rather more authentic. This I did by covering a board with dry cement dust and dripping candle wax onto it to create small craters. The impact of the liquid wax sent out tiny rays of dust and the cold wax could be picked out using a pin to leave a circular impact point.

I was so pleased with the result that I decided to immortalise the moment on film. Now, I'm not much a photographer and I certainly didn't have a clue back then but, seizing the family camera, I clicked away in monochrome at my model on its base, bathed in the rays of the setting sun to produce the most dramatic shadows. I'd recently started work at an advertising agency and asked one of the photographic studios we dealt with if they'd develop my film, which they did, producing one or two 10" x 8" prints as a bonus. These were all somewhat out of focus and, rather disappointed, I left them on a corner of my desk. 'Where did you get these?' asked my department manager. Spotting an opportunity for fame and mischief I made some vague reference to friends in high places. I think it was getting on towards lunchtime before someone smelt the proverbial rat and I confessed... but it was fun whilst it lasted. I'd still recommend the dry powder and wax treatment for creating extra-terrestrial scenes. If you use dry plaster and leave it somewhere sheltered but damp it will even set. Eventually.

Top: Stage one outer engine housings and fins.
Centre: the engine housings and fins, once in place, complete stage one.
Bottom: Stage two engine assembly.

Revell's 1:96 *Lunar Module* was a fairly basic build but, with a little work and some wrapping of the lower section and legs in gold leaf, it came together reasonably well; what it didn't do was fit within stage three of the *Saturn V*. Now this might have been my error but no amount of juggling would get it to sit in its designated spot so, in the end, I opted for the version with landing legs extended. The main landing engine bell was shown in the instructions but not included in the kit and, in my search for this, I came across a single sheet of paper printed in black on red. Unfortunately it was in German and my knowledge of that language is more or less limited to ordering drinks. I got the first line: 'Attention: please note' and saw that the text referred to the missing component and one of the others, specifically the landing legs. Off I set to the local library to find a German/English dictionary and there, by happy chance, encountered a real, live German. This kind chap (a

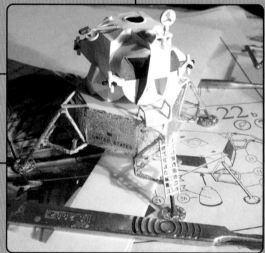

teacher at the local high school) puzzled over the text and concluded that it was informing the reader that the designated parts were either not included in the kit or should be ignored. Well, one wasn't there but, equally, one was, so that's still a bit of a puzzle. The section of the model within which the *LEM* was supposed to sit featured a clear panel so that it could be viewed in position. Being redundant on my build, this was given a coat of primer and airbrushed white to match the exterior of the booster stage.

The *Command* and *Service Module* sections were supplied moulded in a silver grey plastic which had a number of fine, discoloured seams running through it, so I painted the lot in *Vallejo* natural steel and oily steel. The final stage of construction was the *Escape Tower*, which clipped quite securely atop the *Command Module* and that, as they say, was that. Each stage and section of the model is designed to separate to display the various wonders within and this would make a great interpretive tool for anyone involved in education that needed to cover the topic. As a kit it's – well… not bad but very much of its time.

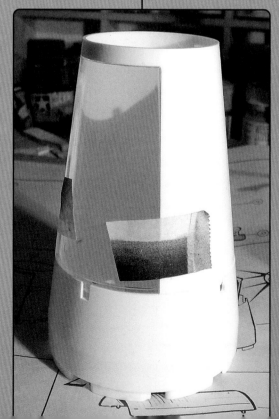

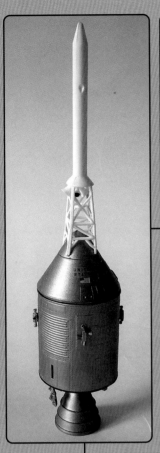

Opposite top: Stage three engine. Opposite centre left: *Service* and *Command modules* plus *Escape Tower*. Opposite centre right: *Lunar Module* in progress. Opposite bottom: Clear panel for viewing *LEM*, subsequently painted white.

This page: the completed model broken down into its separate stages.

Editor's Note: A further re-release of the 1:96 Revell Saturn V is currently available, having been recently issued in March, 2009, with the addition of paints, a brush, glue, and a '40 Years' anniversary roundel to the box art.

One Very Small Step

Modelling 'The Eagle' for Dangerous Films'

MOONSHOT

Article by Mike Tucker

I'm very grateful to my parents who, on the night of 21st July 1969, woke me up, sat me down in front of the black and white television in the front room and made me watch as Neil Armstrong became the first human being to set foot on another planet.

I'm equally grateful that they made me a scrapbook of every newspaper clipping, front page and colour supplement that they could get their hands on, not just because it's a fabulous record of an historic event, but because it was fantastic reference when I came to work on **Moonshot**, a 90-minute film produced by *Dangerous Films* to mark the 40th anniversary of the first of the moon landings.

Dangerous Films director, and visual effects supervisor, Tim Goodchild, had mentioned the project to me whilst we were working on the Emmy-nominated effects for **Human Body – Pushing the Limits**. Originally Tim had hoped to build very large-scale models of both the *Lunar Lander* and the *Command Module* and shoot the descent and landing as 'in camera' sequences. I started to cost up the possibilities of building the models at 1/6th or 1/4 scale – at one point even investigating as to whether we could utilise the moulds made by *Hunter Gratzner Industries* for the Tom Hanks mini series **From the Earth to the Moon** – but, as both the script and budget progressed, it became obvious that building the models at that scale was both unrealistic and unnecessary.

When production eventually commenced it was in Eastern Europe, and I figured that any chance of getting involved was over, but in the summer of 2008 I had a call from Tim asking how quickly we could build a model of the *Lunar Excursion Module* (*LEM*) to ship out to the studios in Lithuania.

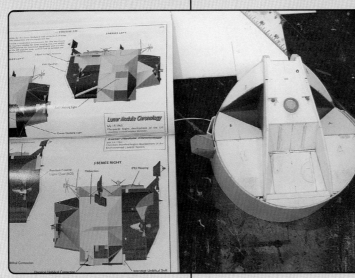

The model was not to be used for filming as such, but was to be photographed in suitable lighting conditions so as to form the basis for a series of digital matte paintings. Tim initially wanted to see if we could super-detail a 1/32nd scale model that was available off-the-shelf. However, having looked at the figures, I was confident that we could provide a much more detailed 1/18th scale model within the budget available.

Top: A rough assembly of the two main sections of the *LEM* to determine proportions.

Centre: Fine tuning those proportions using the *Virtual LEM* book.
Bottom: The upper body now has 'distressed' panelling detail added.

With the bulk of my crew being of a similar age to me, and most having a keen interest in space modelling, I had no shortage of volunteers asking if they could help with the build of this particular model. In the end Nick Sainton-Clark was my choice, not least because he had just completed a series of display models based on the *Eve Online* computer game and had set up a very effective pipeline for creating parts as 3D digital models using *NewTek*'s *Lightwave* software and getting them mass produced at a company called *Arrk* via stereo lithography. That process seemed ideal for both the manoeuvring thrusters and the four, spider-like legs of the *LEM*.

Armed with my vintage scrapbook and the outstanding *Virtual LEM* book produced by *Apogee Books* we set about drawing up a scale plan. With only two weeks to get the model finished and on a plane, Nick and I elected to hit the ground running, working very long hours from day one to try and break the back of the construction and leave ourselves plenty of time to deal with the dressing and fine detail.

With the *LEM* comprising of two parts it was relatively straightforward to progress the upper and lower sections separately, building up the basic structures in *Foamex* and styrene sheet. We were able to work quite quickly at this stage, as not only was the actual spacecraft disturbingly slapdash, but the final model would

Top left: Nick Sainton Clark modelling the legs using *Lightwave* software.
Top right: The resin legs as they arrived from *Arrk*.
Below: Checking that the legs fit the main body.
Bottom: Adding foil and detail to the resin legs.

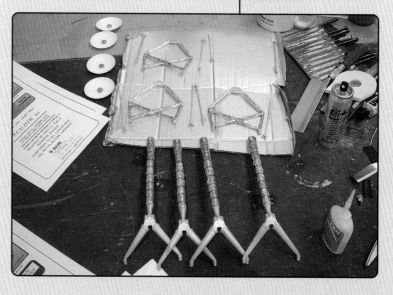

Top: The finished legs are attached to the main body.

Above: A rough assembly to check that all the disparate parts actually fit where they were meant to.

have a good percentage of its surface area covered in foil.

Those foil surfaces were initially of some concern. The wrinkle patterns are very distinctive on the *LEM* and we needed to ensure that we picked a foil that would fold in an appropriate manner to ensure that the scale of the model held up on camera. In the end we used a combination of very thin *Bare Metal* foils applied over a considerably thicker metalised foil used in lighting. The thicker foil provided the correct frequency of wrinkles, whilst the thinner foils – in a variety of subtle changes of colour – gave a more realistic finish.

Once the base section was blocked out it gave Nick the dimensions he needed to begin modelling the legs. These were designed so that each piece had a lug and corresponding socket modelled into the basic shape. In theory this meant that the returned pieces would just plug together and then fit straight onto the body of the model with no further work. Once the sections of one leg were built they were duplicated and the files were emailed over to *Arrk* for them to start making the final versions.

With that process now out of our hands work resumed on detailing the upper and lower sections of the *LEM*. This included the ladders, disc antennae, aerials and the main thruster, all constructed from a combination of custom made vacuum form shapes and *EMA* parts. At this point, confident that we had the bulk of the model blocked out, and with the stereo lithography parts underway, we actually slowed our pace slightly, a welcome reversal of the way that jobs usually go!

The second week started with the arrival of the legs and thrusters. As always with this particular process there is a certain amount of clean up that is necessary, but, as with the main body of the ship, the foil covering would ultimately hide a multitude of sins. Once again, care was taken to ensure that the scale and frequency of the wrinkles of the foil on the legs matched the reference photographs, this time utilising tissue paper as an underlying base with the thin *Bare Metal* foils on top. Thin lining tape was then wound around the legs to create the bands.

Nick's technique of modelling in lugs and sockets worked perfectly and the only additional work that was needed was to produce the footpads. These were, again, produced as vacuum formed parts from a turned plaster plug and attached to the legs with an *EMA* joint.

From the very start it had been doubtful that the model would be self-supporting and, as a result, a metal rod was inserted through the main thruster. This rod screwed through to the baseboard, supporting the weight of the model for both shooting and transport purposes. Some discussion was had about what colour the rod should be painted for ease of removal once the photographs had been taken. In the end it was simply painted black.

Upper sections of the ship were clad in thin styrene sheet, twisted and buckled slightly to recreate the stress patterns visible in all our reference. Most of these panels were pre-painted, then cut and fitted, avoiding a long winded and complicated masking job. Our reference indicated that much of the *LEM* was a light green in colour, but a lot of the photographs of it in space showed it as very reflective. In the end we solved this discrepancy by giving the green panels a thin coat of varnish so that they created very bright highlights when lit.

Silver surfaces were masked and sprayed, and the decals enlarged from various reference photographs and then cleaned up and resized in *Photoshop*.

Our final job was to build a sturdy crate so that the model would survive

Top: The manoeuvring thrusters and blast shields are glued into place.
Above: Antennae detail.
Opposite top left: Foil detail is added by Mike Tucker to the underside of the ascent stage.
Opposite top right: The access ramp is fitted.
Bottom: The completed model prior to being crated up.

its plane trip to Lithuania. As is always the way with anything sent by air the crate weighed nearly four times as much as the model, but with a crew at the other end dependant on the model arriving in one piece it was better to be safe than sorry.

The model was ultimately shot on the moon surface set as a series of high resolution still images. These were used as the basis for the digital matte paintings executed by Tim Goodchild and then passed over to Hayden Jones at *Rushes* who handled the final compositing as illustrated on the first page of this article.

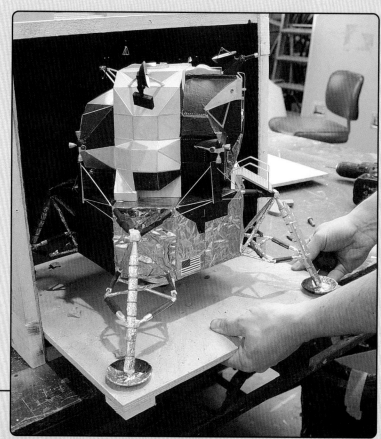

Right: Crating up ready for shipping.
Below: Nick Sainton Clark and Mike Tucker pose with the model in the workshop at Ealing.
Opposite: The completed model.

CREDITS

MOONSHOT

A **Dangerous Films Production** for **ITV 1** and **The History Channel**
Director: Richard Dale
Visual Effects Supervisor: Tim Goodchild
Miniatures: Mike Tucker *and* Nick-Sainton Clark
Digital Effects: Hayden Jones

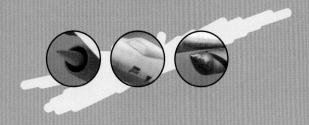

'Tested to destruction'
Special Hobby's X-15A

Article and photographs by Gary R. Welsh

On October 3rd, 1967 Pete Knight climbed into the *X-15A* and set off on what would be the aircraft's last test flight. The *X-15* program had been an extraordinary success story for *NASA* up to that point, helping in the development of throttle control rocket motors (the *X-15A* was powered by the revolutionary *Thiokol LR-99*) and space suits, and generating an extraordinary amount of data on the thermodynamics of high-mach-number flight. Although classed as an experimental aircraft, pilots of the *X-15* were awarded astronaut's wings for any flight over the altitude of 62 miles, so technically the *X-15* can be regarded as the world's first 'space plane'.

Pete Knight had set the absolute speed record in the *X-15A* the previous year on November 18th, 1966 at 6.33 mach (or 4,250 mph) thanks to the addition of ablative coating *MA-25S* – a resin base, catalyst and glass bead powder mixture developed by *Martin Marietta* that protected the airframe from the extreme heat generated by the friction of flying at high-mach-numbers through atmosphere. Today's flight was different, however – today Knight would push the *X-15* to its design limits.

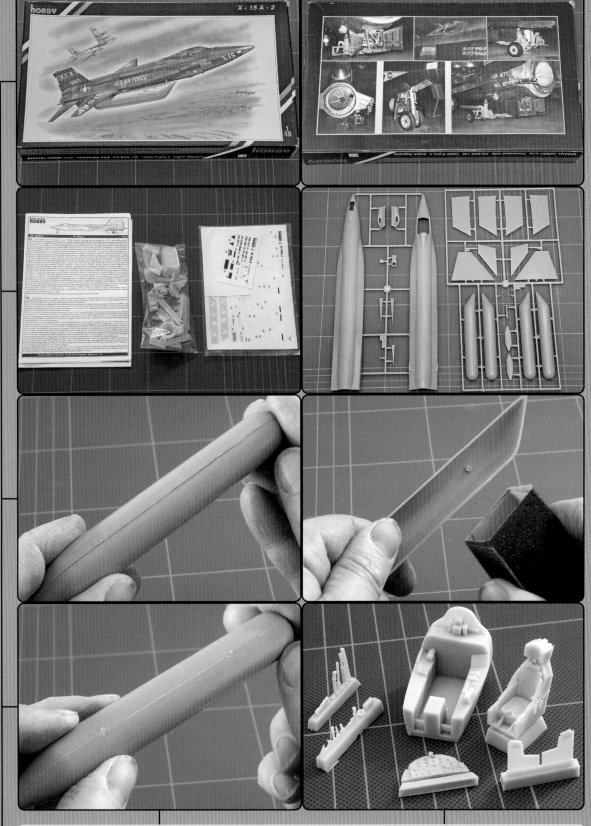

Top row: Box Art for the original *X-15A* release—the rear of the box showing the reference shots that proved to be invaluable during construction. Second row: Basic instructions, a bag of resin goodies and superb quality decals finish the package. The basic sprues—the parts are well moulded, with very delicate panel line detail. Third row: This shot shows the basic fit of the kit. Although alarming this is normal for limited run model kits. The bonding surfaces of the parts are sanded flat to improve the fit. Bottom row: This shot shows how the fit of the parts has improved. The wonderful cockpit resin parts, unfortunately not needed for the ablative version.

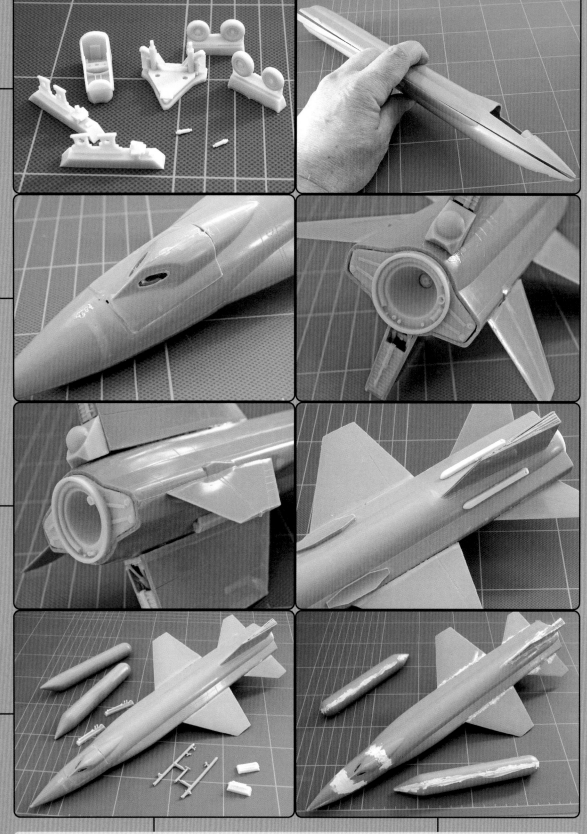

Top row: Ground handling trolly and undercarriage are also catered for in resin. Again, these are not needed for the ablative version. Image shows how warped the fuselage parts are, requiring clamping to get a good fit. Second row: The canopy is designed to be modelled in the open position – hence the bad fit of the parts. A rear shot showing the gaps around the model once construction is complete. All needed careful filling and sanding. Third row: The very evident gaps around the tail area. The wing to fuselage fit isn't too bad. Bottom row: Basic construction completed – the detail parts are still attached to their pouring blocks. Lots of filler- round one!

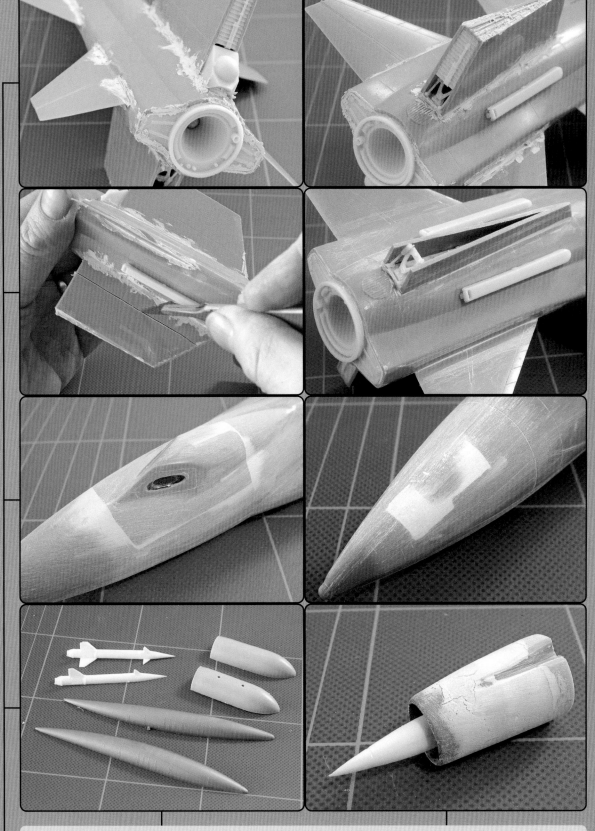

Top row: Rear shots show the amount of filler needed. Second row: Removing the lower tail using the back end of a scalpel to gently score through the plastic in a controlled manner. With the tail removed a bulkhead must be fabricated to enclose the resin detail. Third row: After lots of work the canopy finally looks as if it's a perfect fit. The forward undercarriage doors are obliterated by the filling and sanding process. Bottom row: The parts needed to make a scramjet. The completed scramjet unit ready to be fitted.

Take-off proceeded without a hitch and within an hour the *X-15A* (slung under the port wing of a *B52*) was at release altitude and Knight began pre-flight checks. Following engine ignition and release, Knight adjusted the angle of attack to 15 degrees then pitched the aircraft to 35 degrees and dropped the tanks at mach 2. When the aircraft had reached 99,000 ft Knight decreased the angle of attack by 6 degrees and entered the maximum speed segment of the flight. Engine shutdown occurred at 6,630 ft per second 6.7 mach (4,520 mph). Unofficially this was a new world record. The flight had gone seemingly without a hitch, although Knight had reported that pitch control was very sensitive and he had had trouble holding a constant angle of attack. In addition to this the fight profile had wandered slightly off plan.

Post flight analysis of the airframe revealed substantial damage to the *MA-25S* coating, however, making it impossible to repair. Further investigation found that the airframe itself had also suffered serious damage and that the dummy scramjet mount had failed. In fact, so much damage had been inflicted on the airframe that it was decided that the aircraft should be grounded permanently and handed over to the Airforce Museum services for static display. Stripped of its ablative coating and repainted in its original black scheme, this extraordinary machine resides today in the *Smithsonian Institution*'s *National Air and Space Museum* – fittingly, next to the Wright flyer.

Construction

The *X-15A* was produced as a model by *Monogram* and *Revell* during the original flights and both have been reissued on a number of occasions since. However, *Special Hobby* really did the subject the justice it deserved with the release of their 1/48th kit *X-15A* in 2003. As a 'limited run' kit this initial release quickly sold out, prompting *Special Hobby* to issue two further 1/48th kits (with and without dummy scramjet) as well as two 1/32nd versions and a 1/72nd version (under the *MPM* label), all of which are still available.

The subject of this article, one of the initial release *Special Hobby* kits, is a mixed media affair. A large, end-opening box features striking artwork of an *X-15A* improbably landing with its external fuel tanks still attached, and with a handy, brief photo essay of the preserved aircraft on the rear. Two limited run injection sprues with delicately recessed detail contain all the major parts, whilst a hefty bag of resin – or PUR – detailing and a cracking decal sheet by *Progateam* round off the package.

Limited run models require a little more attention than standard injection kits. However, if care is taken in preparing the parts they should present no problems for the skilled injection modeller.

I began by washing both injection part trees in hot water to which I had added a squirt of washing-up liquid. Short run kits are usually coated in a release agent, so removing any trace of this is critical to ensuring that the paint adheres to the plastic later on. Once these had been rinsed and dried I continued by removing all the major parts from their trees. The gates on the sprues are rather large and require care to separate. The mould gates and ejection pins were removed with a sharp scalpel blade and the glue face edges sanded flush with wet and dry wrapped around a block (see photo). All parts were then test fitted and any adjustments made. The trick to building short run kits and vac-forms is to make a plan and stick to it. Do this and you shouldn't come a cropper.

At this stage the major components were glued together without much trouble. The kit's resin detail parts were next to be dealt with and these were washed and dried as per the injection trees. A superb level of detail is provided for the cockpit but, unfortunately, none of this would be seen as I was building the ablative-coated version which has its cockpit covered by coated shutters, so all this exquisite detailing was superfluous to requirements and ended up in the spares box. Other resin detail was removed from its pouring block using a scalpel, the blade gently scoring through the resin attachment sliver over many passes. Any trace of the attachment was then removed with a small, flat jeweller's file.

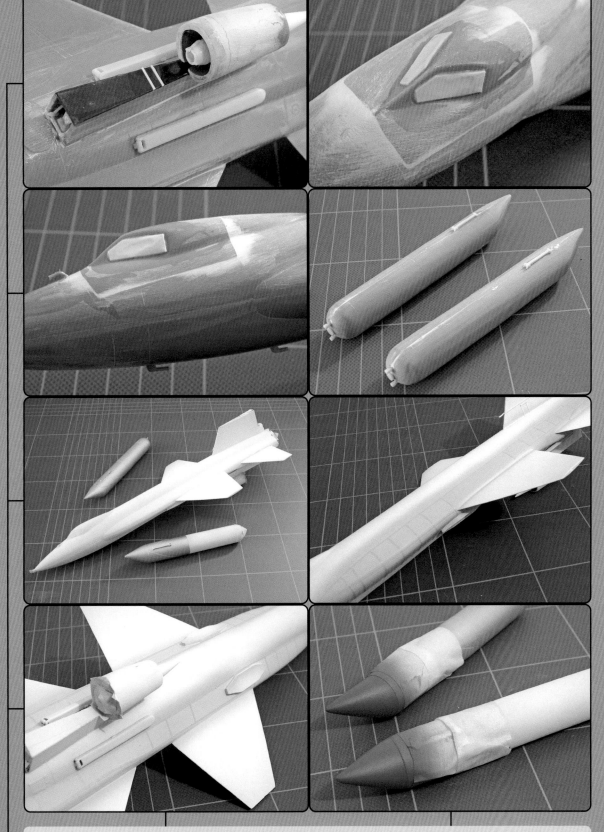

Top row: The scramjet and bulkhead fitted and blended in with more filler. Ablative shutters are added to the model made from 10 thou *plasticard*. Second row: The final injection parts are added. Resin detail is finally added to the fuel tanks. Third row: The main matt white has been applied – note aluminium on the fuel tanks. Silver-grey panel lines are carefully masked. Bottom row: Underside view of masked silver-grey panel lines. Fluorescent red is added to the tips of the tanks.

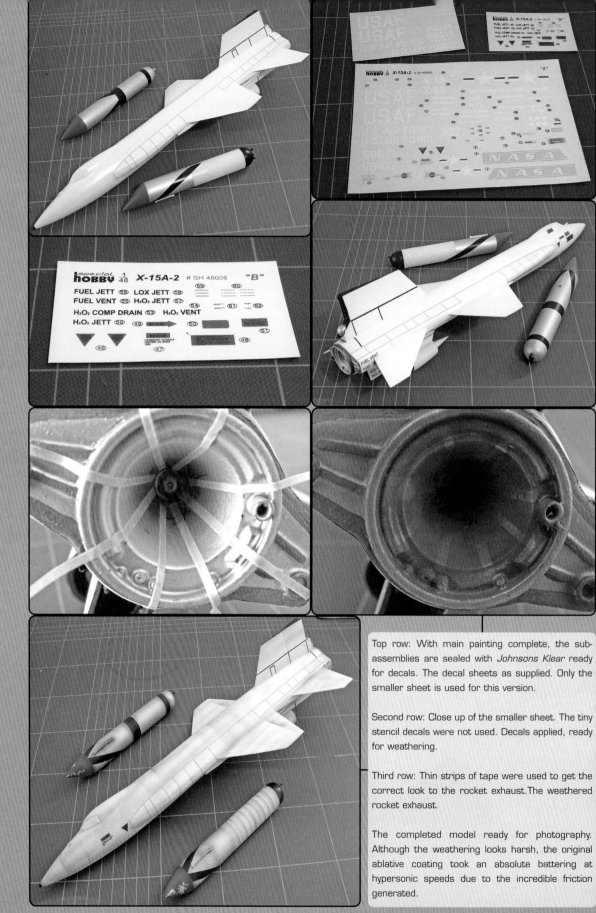

special hobby $\frac{1}{48}$ **X-15A-2** # SH 48008 "B"

FUEL JETT 56 LOX JETT 58
FUEL VENT 55 H₂O₂ JETT 57
H₂O₂ COMP DRAIN 53 H₂O₂ VENT
H₂O₂ JETT 52

Top row: With main painting complete, the sub-assemblies are sealed with *Johnsons Klear* ready for decals. The decal sheets as supplied. Only the smaller sheet is used for this version.

Second row: Close up of the smaller sheet. The tiny stencil decals were not used. Decals applied, ready for weathering.

Third row: Thin strips of tape were used to get the correct look to the rocket exhaust. The weathered rocket exhaust.

The completed model ready for photography. Although the weathering looks harsh, the original ablative coating took an absolute battering at hypersonic speeds due to the incredible friction generated.

The resin detail was added and here the inclusion of the photo reference came into its own, as I found I was constantly referring to it as the exact placement of the detail parts in the instructions is a little on the vague side.

Once construction was complete I removed the bottom of the tail using the back edge of a scalpel. I then fabricated a bulkhead and had a rummage through my spares box to find suitable parts for the scramjet. If you have the original version of this kit and want to represent Pete Knight's record breaking flights you will have to add this feature. I think *Aries* originally produced a resin add-on for this kit, but I was unable to locate one so had to cobble the component together referring to reference I had in the form of Martin Jenkin's superb *The X-planes* book. The completed scramjet was then added to the bottom of the bulkhead.

After a few days of careful filling, sanding, refilling and re-sanding (par for the course when making short run injection kits) I added the final mix of injection and resin details to the kit. I also constructed and applied cockpit shutters cut from 10thou *plasticard*. At this point I would usually re-scribe any lost panel detail. However, the ablative coating on the *X-15A* was so thick that this was really unnecessary, except for the main flying surfaces.

The painting process began by treating everything to a generous coat of *Hycote Matt Black* to give the colours that were to follow a scale look. I then masked off the black panel lines and markings on the fuel tanks before spraying *Hycote Aluminium* where needed. This was then masked off and the whole model given a thorough coat of *Hycote Matt White* prior to it being put aside to harden.

Once the model was properly dry the detail painting was added. *Liquitex Fluorescent Red* was sprayed onto the tips of the tanks, finishing them off except for weathering. The main body was then sprayed *Vallejo Silver-Grey* and the panel lines carefully masked with thin tape. The overspray was then eliminated with more *Hycote Matt White*. With all masking removed everything was sealed in with several coats of *Johnsons Klear/Future* in preparation for the decals.

Special Hobby provide superb decals… unfortunately only a small sheet is needed for the ablative version. I added these with no problems at all, but chose to leave off the smaller stencils as these would all but disappear once the model had been properly weathered.

Weathering was carried out with *Paasche*'s *Talon* airbrush using *Vallejo Black-Grey* and *Field-Tan*. The ablative coating on the *X-15A* was very high maintenance and, as I was going to depict mine 'in action', I gave my model an in-flight, battered appearance. Details were picked out using a brush and then softened with the airbrush. The shutters were highlighted in pure white to make them a focal point on the model. Following a solid coat of matt varnish the model was finished.

Special Hobby's *X-15* kits are superb and really capture this astounding aircraft in a way no other manufacturer does. Granted, they are not kits for the beginner and require a lot from the builder to generate an acceptable finished model. All that extra love and attention is rewarded, however, with a near faultless representation of one of the most important subjects in the development of manned space flight.

The *X-15A* accelerates to mach 3 where the external fuel tanks will be jettisoned.

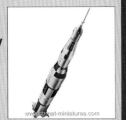
37

The Real Stuff

A look back at the making of
Philip Kaufman's classic
'The Right Stuff' 25 years later

Article by Paul Taglianetti

I n 1979 Tom Wolfe's biographical account of the United States' post-war experiments with rocket-powered, high-speed aircraft was released in America. **The Right Stuff** became a smash best seller, presenting in explicit detail the stories of the first *Project Mercury* astronauts selected for the *NASA* space program. Wolfe spent years doing extensive research and interviewing test pilots, the astronauts and their wives, and the renowned *Mercury Seven* and their families. The book's in-depth journalism revealed to the reader the insights of those brave early test pilots and examined the personal strength and courage needed to undertake such dangerous exploration. The success of Wolfe's book made it a ripe property for a Hollywood interpretation. A renewed national interest in the space

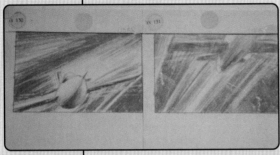

program had emerged due to the US shuttle-based missions, together with a revitalisation in popular fiction of the depiction of space travel due to the **Star Wars** films and their contemporaries. Bay Area filmmaker Philip Kaufman, whose iconoclastic resumé includes the underrated cult film **The Wanderers** and the 1978 remake of **Invasion of the Body Snatchers**, as well as an adaptation of Milan Kundera's novel *The Unbearable Lightness of Being*, took up the challenge of adapting Tom Wolfe's book.

For his crew, Kaufman gathered some of the Bay Area's most talented filmmakers, including renowned cinematographer Caleb Deschanel, best known for his work on **The Black Stallion** and **The Natural**. The film's considerable effects concerns were handed over to Bay Area visual effects expert Gary Gutierrez. Absolute realism and faithfulness to the experiences of the pilots depicted in the film were foremost on Kaufman's mind and Gutierrez began by storyboarding the flight sequences so that planning and budgeting could commence. 'I had done storyboarding for Carol Ballard for **The Black Stallion** and then ended up doing the poster for the movie and the title sequence design,' recalls Gutierrez. 'Then Phil (Kaufman) was looking for someone to storyboard the movie. Ballard recommended me to Phil, I met with him and he basically told me what he needed. He had a script that he'd written but he had to make a presentation to Alan Ladd, Jr. at the *Ladd Company*. [He] felt that the best way to present it was through the storyboards in order to get the financing for the picture, so he hired me and *Colossal Pictures*, my company. I formed a separate company, *US Effects,* which was just formed to create the effects for that movie.'

Gutierrez began by doing extensive research into the historic craft used for early space exploration, as well as drawing detailed boards of the effects sequences. Recalls Gutierrez, '[Kaufman] asked me to storyboard the effects sequences. Production already had done a considerable amount of research themselves, which we got access to. The father of one of my assistants used to work for *Bell Aircraft* and she got us a lot of information. Chuck Yeager was a consultant while we were doing the storyboards and basically explained what happened. Yeager used to say, "Well, that's what *really* happened, but I know you fellows have to flower it up." So we storyboarded the movie in great detail – myself and two or three assistants. Tim Bauxell, an artist at *Colossal*, was my primary storyboarding collaborator. We ended up doing about 1,800 drawings total, that told the story from the title sequence to the ending. We took the storyboards down to Los Angeles for a meeting with Alan Ladd, Jr. Phil had set up a large room there at the *Ladd Company* with dining tables spread all around the perimeter of the room, and we laid

Top: Some 1,800 drawings were created to storyboard the movie from its title sequence to the ending.
Above: Examples of Gutierrez's storyboards for **The Right Stuff**.

out the first batch of storyboards all around it. Phil then started outlining the movie to Alan Ladd, Jr. using the boards as he walked around the room. As he would finish a couple of the tables we would start filling in the next round.'

Eschewing the popular motion control technology so prevalent in the effects-heavy films of the time, Gutierrez and his crew created some of the most visually engaging and emotionally gripping visual effects images of the period. Gutierrez: 'Certainly the hot thing at the time, the prevailing paradigm, was blue screen motion control. That was what *Boss Films* and *ILM* were doing. It seemed obvious that there was going to need to be some amount of motion control, particularly for the space sequences. In our initial tests we also did some blue screen tests with an *X-1*, which is orange against blue and makes a pretty good matte. And so we did some tests and they were time-consuming. With motion blur and getting that down we were able to get a pretty convincing shot. When Phil saw it he thought it was cool but the problem was that when you're doing motion control you're generally prescribing exactly what the choreography is going to be.'

Many of the historic aircraft for the film would have to be recreated with great fidelity. Amongst them was the *BELL X-1*, the experimental jet flown by pilot Chuck Yeager that broke the sound barrier on October 14th, 1947. To give the viewer the impression of great speed during Yeager's historic flight, Gutierrez and his crew went through considerable trial and error to achieve a realistic look for the forward motion of the *X-1* as it speeds through the upper atmosphere. Gutierrez decided that 'in-camera' techniques would create the most dramatic and realistic sense of speed and scope, and could achieve the convincing effect that Kaufman was looking for. 'I remember

feeling a lot of resistance. A lot of guys that worked there were from *ILM* and I was new to the nature of big things like that and it was daunting to get them to think outside of the box a little bit because blue screen was just the hippest thing and you should be able

Top and centre: the *US Effects* team shoots the *Friendship 7* re-entry.

Above: Gutierrez prepares the *X-1A* for photography.

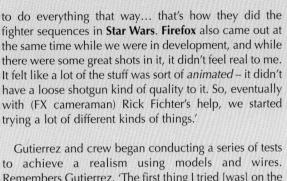

to do everything that way… that's how they did the fighter sequences in **Star Wars**. **Firefox** also came out at the same time while we were in development, and while there were some great shots in it, it didn't feel real to me. It felt like a lot of the stuff was sort of *animated* – it didn't have a loose shotgun kind of quality to it. So, eventually with (FX cameraman) Rick Fichter's help, we started trying a lot of different kinds of things.'

Gutierrez and crew began conducting a series of tests to achieve a realism using models and wires. Remembers Gutierrez, 'The first thing I tried [was] on the third story of this building and I had a bunch of guys go down on the street behind the building beneath our window and hold a parachute. There were about a dozen crew guys down there holding a parachute to catch the model, like somebody jumping out of a burning building. I took our $6,000, six-foot *X-1A* model and, holding it with my hand out the window, I dropped it, and it kind of flew a little bit and they caught it. Cameraman Rick Fichter was standing directly under, looking back to the building and out towards the sky. He thought that looked pretty good and we tried it again and again. After about three tries I couldn't risk it any more. When Phil saw that in dailies he just flipped – he thought, *that's it!*'

Although great attention was paid to historic accuracy in every shot, some creative liberties were taken with a few effects, as Gutierrez remembers: 'Phil wanted the *X-1* to do a sort of victory roll, which Chuck, as I recall, said that he didn't do and would never do – it was a show-off thing to do and, as much as he has a reputation for being kind of a cowboy, a loose cannon, he's not. He's very by the book and was always saying that he really did fly by the book. That's his story and he's sticking to it. But Phil wanted this victory roll, so we took

Top: Matte painting of Earth in progress.
Centre: the *Bell X-1* miniature is filmed on set.
Bottom: Mark Stetson adds the finishing touches to the *Friendship 7* module.

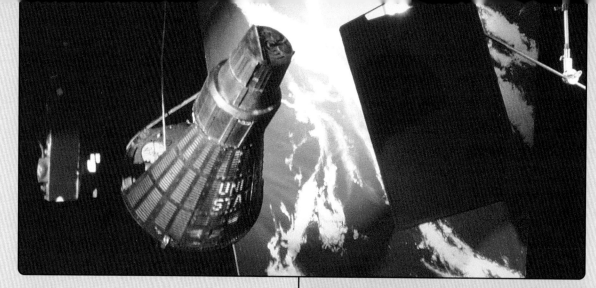

our 3-foot *X-1* model and stretched it between [two guys]. If you can picture those kites where the guy has a bar and the kite has a string coming from [it, so the controller is] more like a puppeteer… There was one guy on each end of the plane, one at the tail, one at the head, attached to the plane through wires running through the wings and the body. They stretched these out between them so that the plane was on invisible wires and a cameraman was underneath them. Then they would just sort of puppeteer this floaty motion and twist their bars over. It was coordinated so as to make it flip over and right itself and settle. And I bet we did 30 takes at high speed, shooting probably 96 frames a second, so that the faster they did it the smoother it could be.'

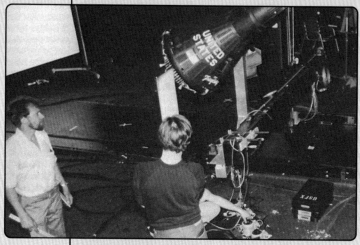

The *Friendship 7* miniature being photographed at *Colossal Pictures'* studio in the Bay Area.

Creating so many miniatures, which would have to perform stunts, be hung on wires or exploded, required an experienced model/miniature designer. 'My initial model shop had this guy named Frank Morelli who had worked with me for many years as a model maker for *Colossal*,' recalls Gutierrez. 'He made a prototype of the *NF104*, but he really was not familiar with the requirements and I was ignorant in some respects and sort of let him run with that ball. But it was too heavy and it [looked] really cool but it was not workable. He created the space capsule as well. He did a great job on that, but it was also too heavy. Eventually I brought in Mark Stetson to run the model shop because it was really a bigger deal than Frank was capable of handling, although he was a great artist and contributed a lot to the movie. But I needed somebody to manage a much larger group, who really knew what he was doing. We made the models in the traditional way, moulds and so forth, based on the plans that we had.'

Gutierrez and his crew of artists used any methodology or material available off the shelf to achieve a desired effect. 'We made a crossbow catapult with surgical tubing so that we could basically launch a *Revell* model kit of the *NF104*. We must have bought 50 or 60 *NF104* model kits. The model shop did a great job on them but these were all for fast-moving shots that were not close, so they didn't have to be perfect.' Special circumstances would force Gutierrez and his crew to find creative solutions to many of the film's technical issues, such as picking a suitable location in which to shoot the models. Tests concluded that natural light was the way to go, so the *US Effects* team needed wide-open space and clear skylines. 'We did a lot of shooting out in the street behind the studio and on the local streets at first,' Gutierrez remembers. 'It was like an industrial area with very little traffic. We didn't even get permits, we just went out there and shot all the time. But finally I needed to get a place where we could have a clear view of the horizon in all directions without obstruction, and found a hilltop area that was only a mile from our studio, in Hunters' Point in San Francisco. It was a big, open hilltop with nothing around it. We rented the space and it had a clear view of the bowl of the sky, and that gave us a lot more freedom to shoot in any angle at any time of day. And then we'd paint the wires out, sometimes with paint, sometimes with gun blue, and use as thin a wire as we could. Several shots of the *B52* were flying into the sunset… not the takeoff shot, which is an actual piece of stock footage, but once it's in the air it's a model. It was an off the shelf *B29* model kit that had the propellers' motor driven by batteries that we could remotely turn on and off. It was just suspended in the air under some grip stands and, at the right time of day looking into the sunset and with camera motion, it looked like what we had studied in all of the actual air-to-air combat flight test footage. We'd mimic those kinds of motions and it looked real. What's great is you can't see the wires and you've got real light reflecting on an object, interacting with it in the fullest way, and you're using the right focal length and your camera is moving in a way that is authentic, that's actually related to actual stuff that we studied, and it's going to look great.'

Gutierrez recalls the constant wear and tear on the flight models during shooting. 'We had a unit that we called the *MASH* unit, so every time one would get broken or chipped or whatever there was a unit constantly gluing them back together. It was basically the same thing – we were launching these things straight up or in an arc or different ways with a team of parachute catchers running around and trying to catch them, which they usually did but sometimes they missed. So we could shoot directly into the sun with other guys who had had live action experience as second and third cameramen; we could get the shot in-camera against blue sky and with the sun in the background and the sun glints. You have to go a long way in CG to match the sun as your gaffer because it's just direct, collimated sunlight – even on a not very highly finished model it can look very realistic.'

This page and over: *Bell X-1* and *X-1A* models being photographed.

Ultimately the story moves on from Yeager's historic flights to the early training of the *Mercury Seven* astronauts, the visual style switching from the lightning-fast, quick cutting of the Yeager flights to the orbits of the *Mercury Seven* missions.

John Glenn (played in the film by Ed Harris) would be the third of the *Mercury Seven* to be launched into space and the first to achieve multiple orbits around the Earth. Gutierrez and crew used a variety of techniques to accomplish the highly realistic shots of the capsules orbiting the Earth.

During his re-entry, mission control notices a serious problem with the capsule's retro pack heat shield, which comes apart from the spacecraft's hull, but Glenn is able to angle the ship during re-entry to protect himself from the intense heat build-up outside the capsule. Gutierrez: 'The close-ups were done with a really large – about 3½ or 4-foot long – model of John Glenn's *Friendship 7*, so we were going to use the scotch light to in effect over-expose the bottom of the heat shield, to make it really glowing and bright. You do that by positioning the camera relative for your angle, and then put a half-silvered mirror at a 45-degree angle between the lens and the object you're shooting, close to the camera, close to the lens. And at a 90 degree angle to the camera is a light source that is aimed at that mirror, and the light bounces off of the mirror at a 45 degree angle directly to the scotch light and then that light on the scotch light is reflected directly back to its apparent source, which is the mirror, passing through the mirror directly into the lens. It's like having the light shining directly into the lens, except it's bouncing off the mirror, hitting the scotch light and coming directly back into the lens. Then, to get the effect of the stuff burning off of the heat shield, which is designed to burn off as a way of protecting the craft, we left, between the heat shield and the capsule body, a thin slit that went all the way around and we pumped liquid nitrogen into the capsule so it was pressurised and sealed in a way that the only way it could escape was out of these slits that surrounded the heat shield, effectively the edge of the heat shield as it meets the body. Then we had fans positioned to blow that liquid nitrogen directly in line with the directionality of the spacecraft. To achieve the dramatic lighting and heat, we backlit the nitrogen with orange gels to give it a flaming quality and turned on the fans and set the camera. They manually shook the camera in the manner that would replicate the feeling of vibration and all this stuff started blasting around it, and it looked great through the lens.'

Although *Colossal Pictures* disbanded several years ago, Gutierrez continues to work as a visual effects artist, title designer and supervisor in the film industry. 'I'm still in the Bay Area. I have an office at Francis' place in North Beach in (Francis) Coppola's building, *American Zoetrope.*' Gutierrez's career credits include **Flight 93**, **Supernova**, Coppola's **Dracula** and **Top Gun**.

Gutierrez looks back proudly at the work of his team and the overall quality of the final picture. However, he doesn't hesitate to point out things he might have done differently. 'I think the only cringe factor I have in some of the effects that were in **The Right Stuff**

The actual *Mercury Seven* capsule being prepared for launch.

were maybe 3 or 4 of the shots we did on stage that I just think the lighting – the surface of the model was picking up the light and kicks that were out of proportion – showed off the scale, and I think that, as good as we were at guessing how to make stuff work, there were shots that I wouldn't have cut in, but we basically fed everything to Phil (Kaufman). Nothing was filtered, he got everything.'

For Gutierrez, what made **The Right Stuff** such a memorable epic was not just the technical qualities of the film but also the ensemble contributions of all the creative departments, each determined to be faithful to history and the source material.

'That is exactly what made **The Right Stuff** work, because that book is a real eccentric but fascinating and well-documented take on the American space program, from flight tests to John Glenn. There are so many aspects of the book that Phil found filmmaking equivalent ways of doing. The stuff he did by hiring the Bologna brothers is a big part of the Press Corps, which is sort of like a moving unit unto itself. That was a brilliant piece of casting. Those guys portrayed the figures in Tom Wolfe's book he called by various names. I think one [term] was 'Victorian gentlemen', but other times he described it [the corps] sort of like a beast that moved along as if it were an organism. Phil got the way those guys behaved whenever they were going after Grissom or anybody. It was just an insane group, just goofy and funny, and it really captured the spirit of the book. I thought there were so many brilliant things about the way he captured that.

'Ed Harris did a great job. I've always loved that sequence where everybody else is 'tired of monkeys', etc, swearing that they're not going to take this anymore. This is preceding the big shot with the triumphant walk down the hall with the guys in their space suits. Then the music kicks in and there's that great moment [with the guys] marching in solidarity down the hallway, which has been imitated many times, and that brilliant sequence of all the rockets exploding and these guys standing there watching and saying, "You want me to get on top of that?" Phil really brings it home. That's *real*. Those guys really did go out and watch those rockets go up and explode – rockets they were expected to get on within a few months.

'It was a good experience, really great, and I was really proud to be a part of it.'

Special thanks to Gary Gutierrez and Kathie Louy for research and transcription. Photographs courtesy of Gary Gutierrez and the author.

Author Paul Taglianetti is a Visual Effects producer and journalist living in Los Angeles.

The unrealised shape of things to come
Building Revell's 1/288th
Sänger transporter kit

Article and photographs by Gary R. Welsh

E ugen Sänger was born in Hapsburg on the 22nd of September, 1922. After gaining his pilot's wings in 1929, Sänger began to explore the possibilities of using rocket propulsion over propeller-driven aircraft to counteract the drop in efficiency at higher altitudes. Sänger knew that a rocket-powered aircraft could achieve significantly greater ranges at high altitudes over conventional aircraft.

Following four years of study Sänger published his thesis – *The Technique of Rocket Flight* – regarded as an important milestone in the development of liquid-fuelled rocket motors.

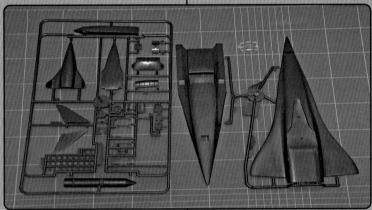

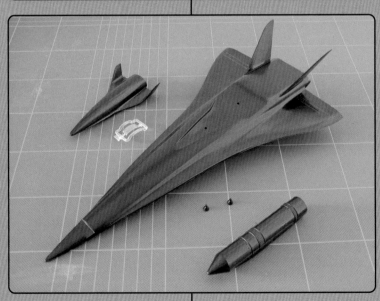

Sänger continued his work on rocket motors, along with mathematician Irene Bredt (who Sänger would eventually marry) throughout the 1930s and '40s, secretly publishing a paper, *Rocket Propulsion of Long-Range Bombers,* in 1942.

Sänger's proposal was simple: A rocket aircraft would be launched on a 1.8-mile long monorail pushed by a captive rocket booster sled capable of producing 600 tonnes of thrust. The 100-ton rocket engine on the aircraft would then propel the bomber to a height of 100 miles (does this sound familiar?) where the aircraft would skip the atmosphere, achieving theoretical ranges capable of bombing the Australian continent. Although work on the Sänger-Bredt *Antipodal Bomber* ceased in 1942 due to the fact that technology at the time was unable to produce metals capable of taking the extreme heat that Sänger predicted the airframe and combustion chamber would have to withstand, Sänger is regarded today as the godfather of the space plane. Even books on NASA's *Space Shuttle* state his pioneering work as its direct descendant.

Post war, he continued his work in Paris with his wife, and his theories were taken up by *Junkers* in the 1960s, producing the *Raumtransporter* proposal, a project that Sänger consulted on. His original space plane concept was somewhat superseded by *NASA's Shuttle* program, however, which was grounded in solid booster technology to achieve orbit.

Dr Eugene Sänger died on the 10th February, 1964.

In the late 1980s the space plane was back on the agenda as the search for the *Shuttle's* replacement began. *NASA* produced the *X-30* proposal

Opposite: The *Mothership* powers into orbit carrying the *Cargus* module.
Top: box art for *Revell's Sänger* kit. Centre: the basic sprue layout. Above: construction is swift, taking around 15 minutes.

(superseded by the *Martin X-33 Venturestar* project), while *British Aerospace* conceived the much undervalued *Hotol* project. The French championed the *Dassault Hermes* in conjunction with the *International Space Station* project, while Germany's *Deutsche Aerospace* revealed a 1/8th mock-up of the *Sänger transonic re-useable space vehicle.*

This concept was way in advance of the other proposals and, although now defunct, offers a tantalising vision of what might have been, consisting of a scram/ramjet trans-atmospheric *'Low Earth Orbit' Mothership* and a smaller, rocket-powered *Manned Cargo Carrier* (*Horus*) or *Unmanned Expendable Cargo Carriers* (*Cargus*). These combinations would take off and land on conventional runways at standard airports. At 275 ft long the *Sänger* would indeed have been a magnificent sight thundering down a runway, the smaller *Cargo Carrier* being around the same size as Russia's *Buran* orbiter shuttle.

Revell produced a 1/288th model of the *Sänger* in 1991, based on the 1/8th mock-up. This model is sadly no longer in production, but can be picked up on the second hand market without too many problems.

Two sprues contain all the parts, the majority of which are for the *LEO Mothership* undercarriage. As I was building 'in-flight' versions most of these parts alas rushed headlong into the spares box. A small clear sprue and a decal sheet round off the package.

Construction took a matter of minutes, as there's not really much to do. The fit of the parts is not the best and a few hours of filler and sanding was definitely on the cards. I made a couple of additions to the model.

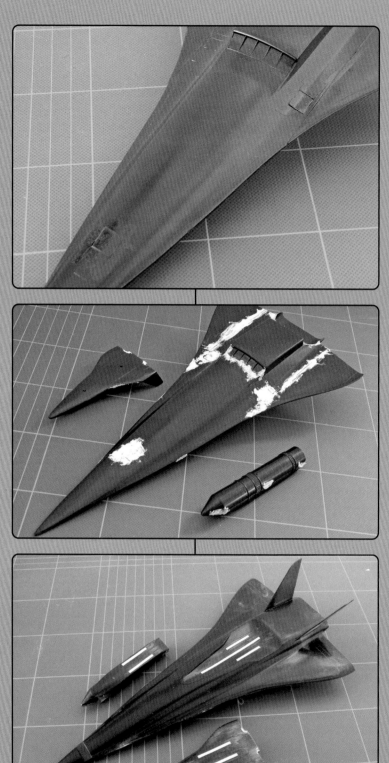

Top: the fit of the parts is not too good. The undercarriage doors are especially bad. Centre: out with the filler, the undersides of the *LEO Mothership* are the worst areas. Above: magnetic clamps are added to the sub-assemblies – purely speculative but they add a sense of realism missing from the kit.

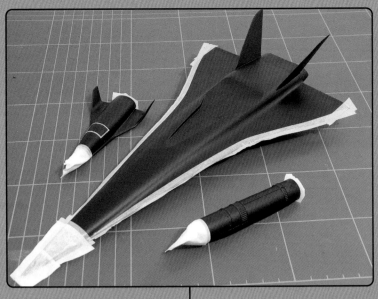

Firstly the *Horus* and *Cargus* smaller rocket engines were replaced with suitably-sized nozzles from *Airfix*'s *Lunar Module* kit. I also added magnetic clamps for each of the vehicles. These are pure speculation on my part, but I felt they were a plausible feature not catered for by the kit.

Following the necessary sanding and filling, everything was given a coat of *Hycote Matt Black*. The black areas of the models were masked off in readiness for their paint.

The *Mothership* was given a coat of *Vallejo Blue-Gunmetal*. *Horus* and *Cargus* were painted with a custom mix of silver, white, French blue-grey and a touch of blue-gunmetal.

Once all the masking had been removed the models were sealed with *Klear/Future* and it was time to add the decals. The kit-supplied waterslides were in an almost unusable state as they had yellowed badly. I remedied this by *Blu-Tac*-ing the sheet to a window for a couple of weeks, which 'bleached' the decals back to a white colour. I then applied them and, as per usual for a *Revell* kit of this period, they were appalling, requiring copious amounts of *Micro Sol* and *Set* to get them down… and still the carrier film refused to disappear.

Following further coats of *Klear* and matt varnish the model was aged using a mix of black, grey and silver that was airbrushed on using *Post-it* notes. This was then followed by steaks of black-grey to simulate burn areas that had accumulated during transonic flight and re-entry, applied freehand.

The main *Horus* and *Cargus* engines were painted with *Liquitex Rich Silver*, the smaller ones with *Testors Brass*.

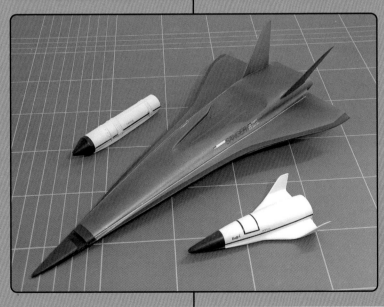

Top: masking off the black areas of the model.

Centre: the kit decal sheet. *Revell* decals from this period are notoriously bad in quality; this kit's offering was no exception!

Above: the decals added ready for weathering.

The cockpit glazing for the *LEO Mothership* was sprayed with *Tamiya Clear Blue*. All these parts were added once painting was completed.

The photographs were shot against an Earth-from-space backing that was painted onto blue card using *Liquitex Ultramarine*, *Medium Blue* and *White*.

It's quite staggering that, as the *Shuttle* is about to be retired, no real alternative has yet to see the light of day. Current *NASA* thinking is centred around updated versions of the long-abandoned *X-20 Dynosaur* project from the 1960s, or the near mythical *Lockheed Martin Venturestar*, neither having yet appeared in prototype form. However, *NASA has* prototyped a full size *X-34 Orbital* and work continues on *NASA's* own *Ram/Scram X-43* space plane.

Revell's kit provides a glimpse of what might have been a viable alternative had sufficient funds been available, capturing the graceful lines of the *Sänger* prototype beautifully.

We can only hope that one day Eugene Sänger's dream of rocket-powered space planes will become a reality.

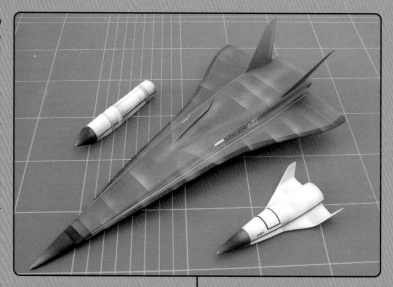

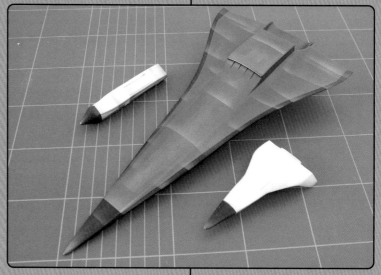

Top: weathering complete. Re-entry scars give a sense of scale and realism.

Centre: the undersides of the weathered models.

Above: detail parts are added, completing the models.

Mission: Moon!

Scratchbuilding the 1947 British Interplanetary Society Moonship

Article and photographs by B. P. Taylor

A history of the *Apollo* program wouldn't be complete without mentioning the work of the *British Interplanetary Society*. Founded in 1933 specifically to evaluate how three astronauts could land on the moon and return safely to the Earth, this group of multi-disciplinary scientists and engineers (whose membership included Arthur C. Clarke) advanced many theories related to spaceflight. They are also credited with designing a lunar landing vehicle in the late 1940s that is generally regarded as the forerunner of the *Apollo Lunar Module*. The result of a great deal of thought and study, the *BIS Moonship* was the first serious attempt to design a specialised craft whose only purpose was to land a crew on the lunar surface.

The lunar mission proposed by the *Society* would begin with the launch of the *Moonship* atop an atomic-powered booster. At an altitude of 500 miles or so it would shed its protective shroud and, with steady thrust from the booster, head toward the moon. Upon reaching lunar orbit, the *Moonship* finally separates from the booster and begins its descent. Moments later, with the *Moonship* now on the lunar surface, an extensive period of exploration by the crew would take place, the conclusion of which would see the return capsule lift off, using the lower part of the vehicle as a launch pad. The capsule would then rendezvous with a tanker in lunar orbit to take on the necessary fuel for the return trip.

With that brief history lesson out of the way I can now get on with a description of

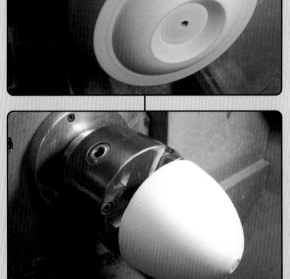

Top: The vacuform pattern for the lower bulkhead is turned on the lathe from *Renshape*.
Above: The pattern for the upper 'return capsule' is turned on the lathe.

how I scratchbuilt a model of this historic spacecraft concept which, surprisingly, has never been released in kit form. But first, it's important on a project such as this to gather as much information as possible in order to get a broad feel for the subject. Although I was previously aware of the *BIS Moonship*, my initial inspiration to build a model of it came from Robert Godwin's *Lunar Exploration Scrapbook – A Pictorial History of Lunar Vehicles*, a fascinating book that's full of lunar spacecraft and vehicle designs generated in the run-up to the *Apollo* program, many of which would make terrific subjects for modellers. In addition to the *Lunar Exploration Scrapbook*, information and images from a number of web sources were also gathered. What quickly became apparent to me was that there seemed to be no definitive version of the *Moonship*. In fact, the paintings and illustrations I found all appeared to vary somewhat in both proportions and details, even those done by the same artist. Confronted with such varied and sometimes contradictory information, I could feel the onset of a condition I call 'option paralysis' – I simply couldn't make up my mind which version to make or which features to include. Fortunately, around this time an *Amazon* purchase showed up at my doorstep in the form of Ron Miller's *The Dream Machines*, a book I'd wanted to add to my reference library for some time. Having no prior knowledge of its specific contents, I was pleasantly surprised to find that it contained a highly detailed, two-view drawing of the *Moonship*, circa 1947, and this would provide all the information I would need to build from.

Getting started

Now that I had a drawing, I needed to determine how large a model I wanted to make, and since the drawing includes both a scale and an astronaut figure, it was a simple matter to enlarge it on the copier to the desired size. I chose to build the *Moonship* at 1/48th scale, which I thought would result in a nice-sized model – not too large and demanding of shelf space, while not too small and easily mistaken for a toy. In thinking how I might approach the model, it seemed pretty obvious that vacuforming would be the best way to create the main components and this would entail a number of lathe-turnings (five, actually) in either low-density urethane foam or *Renshape* to obtain lightweight plastic shells.

Vacuform patterns

I spent an evening turning urethane foam patterns for the tapered lower stage and the bullet-shaped return capsule. The lower stage I decided would be best split into two pieces for a couple of reasons. The first one involves the limitations of vacuforming itself in that this part is so tall that it might have been difficult to get the plastic to draw down over the pattern without 'webbing'. Of course there are ways of preventing this from happening, one solution in this case being to use a large plastic bucket over the pattern and to push down on the softened plastic as it first contacts the pattern, seals on the platen and the vacuum is drawn. The other reason I split the lower portion was that, although it's difficult to tell from the drawing, the lower portion below the break line is angled at approximately six-degrees, while the upper part is at seven degrees. Barely discernable, I know, but it was there and I felt it would be easier to maintain a sharp edge at the transition, which would not have been possible had I vacuformed it as a single piece.

With the patterns for the lower stage of the *Moonship* done, I moved on to the pattern for the return capsule, which was turned out of the same foam. In order to get the proper shape, I used a plastic template so that I could check my progress as I gradually removed material. Unfortunately, a little slip of the chisel caused me to have to put a skim coat of polyester filler over the foam, which was then quickly levelled out on the lathe with coarse sandpaper.

Next up was a pattern for the recessed bulkhead on the underside of the *Moonship*, which was indicated by hidden lines on the drawing. This took much more time on the lathe than the other patterns, being a far more complex shape, although I did take some artistic license and simplify it to make it a bit easier to machine. I used the denser *Renshape* for this particular pattern because, once vacuformed, the side of the plastic sheet drawn against the pattern would be the visible surface on the model. The softer urethane foam would have resulted in a pitted surface and would not have produced as sharp an edge when vacuformed. Once I was satisfied with the overall shape I sanded it with very fine sandpaper, then finished it off with steel wool, which gave the pattern a really smooth, almost polished surface that would in turn be transferred to the vacuformed

Top: the *Renshape* pattern for the lower bulkhead and the resultant vacuform shell. The holes were bored out on a milling machine. Centre: two vacuform shells were derived from urethane foam patterns. Once glued together, they will form the main body of the *Moonship*. Above: the lower bulkhead is glued to the bottom vacuform shell. Polyester filler will be used to blend the two pieces.

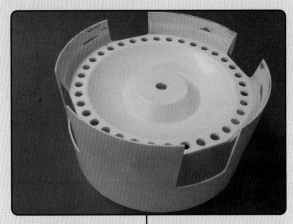

Top: after the lower bulkhead was glued on, cut-outs were machined for additional vacuform pieces that would form the recesses for the rocket motors.

Centre: Metallic lacquers were sprayed onto the main body of the *Moonship*.

Above: vacuformed 'return capsule' before trimming.

shell. A number of tiny holes were then drilled through this pattern to assure that, when vacuformed, the softened plastic would pull tightly against it.

The final vacuform pattern I had to make was for the toroidal structure mounted on top of the return capsule, which I also turned from *Renshape*. At first glance, it would appear that this is supposed to be some sort of docking apparatus, but it does not appear on all reference drawings and, since the *Moonship* was never intended to actually dock with another vehicle, I could only surmise that this was perhaps an instrument module. In fact, running through the centre of this is an instrument that my references refer to as a 'coelostat', which would have been used by the crew for navigational purposes. This elaborate device was designed to compensate for the rotation of the *Moonship*, spun on its major axis to create gravitational forces on the interior walls of the capsule.

Now that the patterns were done, I could commence vacuforming all the main pieces, which I did in a single session. I also pulled an extra set of parts, just in case things went awry. The patterns were removed from the vacuformed *ABS* shells with a loud pop as I used compressed air through a hole drilled in the top. I then marked each piece for trimming using the height gauge, rotating the parts several times against the scriber to establish a trim line that I could then deepen further with an *X-Acto* blade, after which it could simply be snapped off. The trimmed edges were then sanded flat on a sanding board, which is simply a piece of *MDF* with full-sized sheets of sandpaper spraymounted to it.

Lower stage

Before assembling the two tapered vacuforms that make up the lower stage of the *Moonship*, I thought it might be a good idea to machine some *ABS* rings and glue them to the thin shells to not only firm them up a bit, but also to make aligning and gluing them together much easier. I first took measurements off the shells then cut these rings out on a 2-axis programmable milling machine. I then glued them on with plastic solvent. The hatch was located on the upper shell and cut out with a *Dremel*. Fine sandpaper wrapped around a tube smoothed this out, then a disc was solvented in place to represent the hatch itself. I now assembled the two vacuform parts by gluing them together with solvent and holding them firmly together for the short time it takes the solvent to set. After a slight bit of finishing putty was applied and sanded smooth. I added a scribe line slightly below the juncture of the two vacuform shells to avoid the glue joint and putty, which would have made for a nasty line. Rotating the lower stage against the height gauge gave me a shallow groove that I refined with the ground-off back edge of an *X-Acto* blade. At this time I also added some vertical scribe lines that, although they don't appear on the drawing, were done to suggest that the lower part was assembled from pre-fabricated panels.

To add a little more interest to the underside I placed the trimmed vacuform shell for the lower bulkhead back onto its pattern. This was then stuck down to the milling machine with double-sided tape. After locating the centre of this piece, I programmed a series of holes and bored these out. The holes were meant to mimic the lightening holes on the structural rings that are visible in *NASA* footage of the *Saturn V* rocket at stage separation. I pried the shell off the pattern and, after a little cleanup, the bulkhead was glued to the inside of the lower stage with solvent. Polyester filler was used to blend the two together and sanded smooth.

The next task was to machine cutouts on the lower stage into which additional vacuform pieces would be glued to create the recesses for the rocket motors. I first marked these locations in pencil, making sure they were correct with respect to the hatch, then, holding the lower stage in a machine vice, proceeded to remove these areas using a 3/16th inch milling cutter. The vacuform pieces could now be glued into these cutouts with solvent and, once the glue was set, I used flush cutters to remove excess material. More polyester filler was mixed up and pushed into any slight gaps, then sanded flush. With that done I decided to add some detail to the recesses as indicated on the drawing and for this I used *Evergreen* rod and strip. The only other details on the lower stage are the small, corrugated, vent-like details located near the top edge. I made a template for this piece which, rather than being rectangular, had to be adjusted to compensate for the slight curvature of the hull. The template was used to trace the eight vents required onto a textured sheet of plastic, then cut out and solvented in place.

I opted not to include a ladder running down the side of the lower stage of the *Moonship*, even though some of the reference drawings seem to show a rope ladder that would have simply been tossed out the open hatch. It's interesting to note here that the engineers designing the *Apollo Lunar Module* also considered a rope ladder before concluding it to be too unwieldy and potentially dangerous.

Return Capsule

The return capsule is encircled by a ring of small portholes and for these I was able to use some LED lens caps that I found rolling around in one of my storage bins. Although slightly larger in diameter than those shown on the drawing, they seemed to fit the bill, and, of course, saved me from having to make them. The lens caps required that holes be drilled into the capsule and, rather than use an indexing or dividing head on a milling machine, I simply scribed a line on the capsule then laid a narrow strip of tape along it to obtain the circumference through that section of the

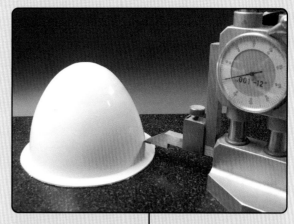

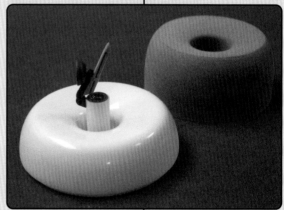

Top: the vacuformed 'return capsule' is marked for trimming with a height gauge. Centre: the upper assembly was created by vacuforming over another *Renshape* lathe-turning. Running through the centre of this structure is a 'navigational instrument' made of styrene tubing and kit parts. Above: LED lens caps were used for the portholes on the 'return capsule'.

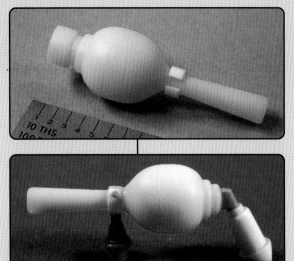

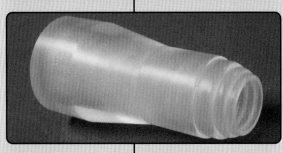

Top to bottom: A single rocket motor was turned on†the lathe from half-inch diameter *ABS* rod. Additional pieces have been added to the rocket motor. This master would then be moulded in *RTV* to produce the twelve castings required for the *Moonship*. The *Moonship*'s exhaust was turned on a lathe from acrylic rod. Close-up of *Moonship* exhaust.

capsule. After removing the tape I marked it with sixteen increments and stuck the tape strip back onto the capsule. At each mark I used a small centre drill first before drilling them out with a 3/16th inch drill bit. Before moving on to the instrument module I added an *ABS* ring to the capsule as I had done to the lower stage to make it a bit more rigid. The last thing I did to the capsule was to machine some material off the top to provide a flat surface for the instrument module.

The instrument module itself was an easy assembly to make. I first added an *ABS* disc to the bottom of the vacuform, then created the supports with styrene rod and strip. The only kit-bashing on this model was used to create the 'coelostat' device that runs through the centre of this assembly. Rummaging through my parts boxes, the pieces that I ended up using to construct it came from aircraft kits and, when done, looked very much like what was on the drawing.

At this point I decided to prime the capsule, lower stage and instrument module, and for this I used a gray automotive primer applied with a spray gun. I then applied some *NitroStan* spot putty to any areas that required attention. Once dry, these areas were sanded and given another light coat of primer. With the surfaces now nice and smooth, I sprayed on a few coats of black lacquer, which would serve as my basecoat. These parts were then set aside to dry thoroughly.

Rocket motors

In the meantime, however, I still had some other important items to take care of. First on the agenda, the main rocket motor for the *Moonship* was turned on the lathe from a length of acrylic rod and, after attaining the proper exterior shape, I bored a hole into it that would later fit a half-inch diameter support rod. As I also do with useful kit parts, I made an *RTV* mould of it, feeling this rocket motor was an interesting enough piece that I might want to use it on some future project. On models requiring a number of the same part or detail, the best approach is to utilise *RTV* moulds and urethane castings whenever possible. Using the appropriate materials and processes for any particular job can certainly make life a lot easier, as well as make you a more productive modeller. Sometimes it's difficult and tedious enough to have to make a single part, let alone a dozen, so I would rely on *RTV* moulds to cast up the rocket motors and landing gear components.

To create a master pattern for the rocket motors I first took measurements with my callipers right off the drawing and machined a single turning on the lathe, holding the half-inch diameter *ABS* rod stock in a collet while I gradually shaped it with lathe bits, files and strips of sandpaper. Final smoothing was done with fine steel wool. The final details added to the rocket motor were some fine grooves, which were done with a lathe bit ground to a fine point. A few bits of piping were then added to the completed lathe turning to match what was on the drawing, then adjusted so that, when fitted into the recesses on the lower stage of the *Moonship*, they would be at the correct angle.

Landing gear

The *Moonship*'s landing gear bears more than a passing resemblance to that of the *Apollo Lunar Module*, no doubt owing to a similar pragmatic engineering approach. Designed specifically for the moon's gravity, it wasn't necessary for the landing gear to support the vehicle's weight on Earth and that would also be true of my 1/48th scale *Moonship*. Even though the vacuform shells are very lightweight, I decided that the model would actually be supported by a rod going up the main rocket motor. The length of this rod would then be adjusted so that the footpads of the *Moonship* just barely touched the display base. I knew when I began this project that the landing gear would provide the biggest challenge to what is otherwise a fairly easy model to make, but using moulding techniques to replicate the pieces was going to make the experience a lot less painful.

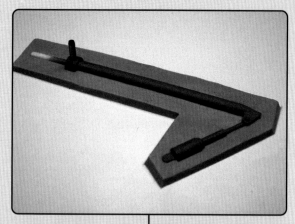

After looking at the drawing for a while I determined the manner in which the landing gear could be broken down for moulding. Making a single master of each of the components, I would then make *RTV* moulds and cast four sets of parts in urethane resin. Fortunately, it worked out that standard or stock rod and tubing could be used to construct the masters. Building right on top of the drawing, the main strut was easily made of styrene rod and tubing. To make the upper and lower supports, aluminum welding rod was easily shaped with pliers until the correct angles were achieved. It took a bit of test fitting and adjusting until I was confident that the various pieces would assemble into an accurate representation of the landing gear. I had to use filler in some areas to take care of some minor gaps that might present problems in moulding, then the parts were sprayed with automotive primer.

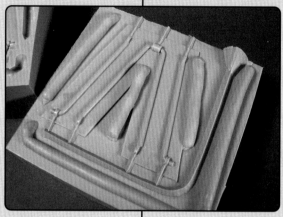

In the final assembly, the landing gear would be attached to U-shaped brackets glued to the lower stage of the *Moonship*. Two different types were required – square brackets for the lower part of the recesses, while the other ones had a slight angle on them to compensate for the curvature on the lower stage. These were machined from square styrene stock, then rivets were added to suggest pivot points.

Top: the main strut is laid up in *Klean Klay* to establish the parting line. Centre: resin castings of landing gear components as they appear upon opening the mould. Brass rod was set into the mould to add rigidity to the thin castings and prevent them from distorting over time. Above: brackets for the landing gear were made of styrene channel, then moulded in *RTV*.

Moulds and castings

With all the masters now ready I began making moulds of the rocket motor, landing gear components and support brackets. The brackets were simply stuck down to a piece of plastic, while the rocket motor and landing gear required two-part moulds and, therefore, a bit more consideration. I very carefully set the masters into *Klean Klay* and, using various

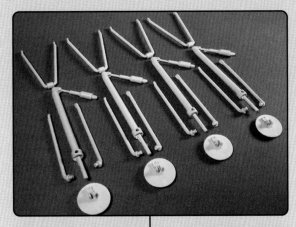

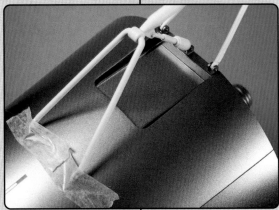

Top: castings required for *Moonship* landing gear.
Centre: resin landing gear components are test-fitted to the main body of the *Moonship*.
Above: view of landing gear and underside detail.

sculpting tools, set about establishing nice, smooth parting lines. Mould boxes were made and the RTV was then mixed, de-aired and poured. Once the first half of the moulds was cured I cleaned off any residual clay then built new containment walls. A light spray of release agent was then applied to the exposed surfaces of the rubber to prevent the two mould halves from sticking together – not a step you really want to forget. I mixed and de-aired another batch of rubber, then poured this into the mould boxes, leaving them to cure. The next evening I separated them, removed the masters, then, using an X-Acto blade, cut in the sprues and vents that would allow the poured resin to flow through the moulds. Although I had incorporated 'snaps' I used rubber bands to hold them securely together. I then proceeded to cast up all the parts I needed, pouring resin into the moulds and setting them into the pressure pot to cure. Because of the delicate nature of the landing gear components, I thought it might be best to set lengths of brass rod into the moulds before closing them up. This I hoped would keep the castings from distorting or sagging over time as resin is sometimes prone to do, especially in thin sections. The support brackets were cast in open moulds with a *Plexiglas* back plate that was waxed to prevent the castings from sticking to it.

I tried to make good use of the time it took the resin to cure by cleaning up the castings as they came out of the moulds – while one set of castings was in the pressure pot I was sanding flash off the previous set. Needless to say, this was the single most time-consuming task on the entire project.

Some of my references of the *Moonship* show it with what are referred to as 'torque jets', while others show no jets at all. I thought the model would look better with the additional rocket motors that in *The Dream Machines* are indicated by hidden lines on the drawing with the notation 'motor position for return take-off'. This required four more castings of the rocket motors, which were modified by removing the piping details then sanded to conform to their position on the lower stage.

After all the castings had been cleaned up I decided to turn my attentions back to the lower stage. By now the black basecoat had been given more than ample time to dry and so I wet-sanded everything with 1000 grit wet-or-dry to provide the smoothest possible surface for the metallic topcoats to follow. I hadn't really given too much thought to the paint scheme, since it seemed as though most, if not all, spaceships of this era (especially in the cinema) were silver in colour. However, I decided to mix up three different metallic shades for the *Moonship* that I felt would make for a less monotone, more visually interesting model. I first sprayed the lower stage of the *Moonship* using the medium metallic. Once that was dry, I used *Nichiban* low-tack tape to mask along the vertical panel lines and sprayed the opposing panels in the darker metallic. Also painted in the darker metallic was the instrument module, while the capsule and main rocket motor were both sprayed silver. While I was at it, I taped off the vent details on the lower stage and sprayed them silver as well.

Assembly

I could now begin to assemble the landing gear components, but before doing so I needed to glue on the pre-painted resin-cast brackets. As I'm disinclined to trust gluing to a painted surface, I carefully scraped away a bit of paint to assure a decent bond. I then stuck each bracket down with a dot of medium *CA*.

Assembly of the landing gear components was carried out on the model itself using tiny amounts of thin *CA* applied with a fine wire. After all four assemblies were made, they were primed and painted with the medium metallic shade. The footpad and lower section of the main strut were also sprayed silver.

With all the fitting that had been done, it should now be a simple matter to glue the landing gear to the lower stage, right? Well, not exactly, as in order to get the supports to stay in the brackets (and five brackets per set), I had to contort my fingers into unnatural positions while the epoxy set. Thankfully, the tubes read '5-minute epoxy' and I only had to do this four times.

The twelve rocket motor castings were each mounted to the end of a toothpick that was shoved into a hole I drilled in the nozzles. After a light spray of primer, I first painted the rocket motors silver and, when that was dry, I masked off the bands on the combustion chambers defined by the fine grooves. These were next sprayed with the medium metallic and, with removal of the tape and painting the insides of the nozzles black, they were ready to be glued on with epoxy.

Before attaching the return capsule to the lower stage of the *Moonship*, I glued the LED lens caps in place by pushing them into the holes, then secured them with a dab of epoxy applied from the inside. At last, the instrument module was glued to the top of the capsule, which was in turn epoxied to the lower stage. As a final touch and in deference to the late Arthur C. Clarke, I added his name to the side of the *Moonship* near the hatch. For this I simply applied individual letters from a sheet of dry transfers available from *Archer Fine Transfers*.

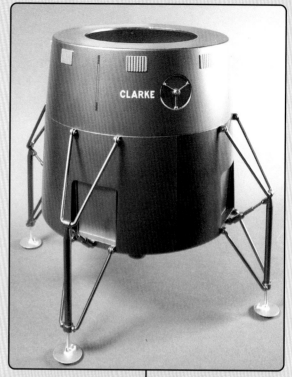

Top: after painting, the landing gear assemblies were carefully epoxied to the resin brackets on the main body of the *Moonship*.
Above: the LED lens caps represent portholes and were epoxied into holes drilled into the 'return capsule'.

Display base

I was now the proud owner of a mint-condition 1947 *Moonship*, but it needed a base on which to display it in the proper setting. I began with a round piece of *MDF*, which established the overall size. A bevelled *MDF* ring was made that was then glued to the base to serve as the crater wall. Polyester filler was used to blend the ring to the base as well as to create some secondary craters. I then used a *Dremel* and a large bit to

introduce some irregularities and striations on the crater wall. I also drilled a half-inch hole into the centre of the base for the support rod. The edge of the base was sprayed with three or four coats of sanding sealer and sanded smooth. I then heavily masked off this edge so that I could coat the surface with a product called *Glaze Coat*, a high-build epoxy coating. I sifted *Woodland Scenics ballast* into the wet epoxy coating, continuing well past the saturation point. The next evening, after the excess ballast had been removed, I glued a few rocks inside the crater and, once all this was dry, the base was painted a suitably lunar gray, given a dark wash, then drybrushed. I decided to sand a flat area onto the base for an *ABS* panel, glued this on, then printed out a nameplate onto a self-adhesive label.

Finally, I thought the display might benefit from having an astronaut included as a scale reference. A 1/48th scale *Apollo* astronaut casting was the basis for this, but required slight modifications, mostly involving reshaping the helmet to more closely resemble the one shown in the drawing. Adding the figure and some equipment cases to the scene you get a much better sense of how large the *Moonship* might have been – roughly twice as tall as the *Apollo Lunar Module*.

Due to the early efforts of the *British Interplanetary Society*, the idea of space travel, and, in particular, a lunar landing, was popularised through increased public awareness, inspiring even more serious thought on the subject. Decades later, *Apollo* mission planners incorporated many ideas originally proposed and developed by the *Society* and their *Moonship* is today seen as having helped point us in the right direction.

Top left: Three different shades of metallic lacquer were used on the model. Top right: the base for the *Moonship* was made of *MDF* and polyester filler. Centre: The completed *Moonship*. Left: *Moonship* on completed base with astronaut and other detailing.

Saturn V three-stage modelling mission—Stage Two:

Complete and Mission Ready

Kitbashing Johnston's Space Centre's display Saturn V in 1/144th scale

Article and photographs by Gary R. Welsh

As I write this feature Barack H. Obama has just been sworn in as the 44th President of the United States of America. It's quite ironic that the subject of this article was brought to us by another iconic President, John F. Kennedy Jnr., the man who decided that America would go to the moon, a project that, as he had predicted, would bring much of the world together in the hope and dreams of a better future. It was the fulfilment of the coming of the age of man. Mankind had decided to go to the moon – *because it could!* The *Apollo* project forged a generation of can-dos, an achievement that echoes with us into the 21st Century.

I was four years old when Neil Armstrong and Buzz Aldrin, the crew of *Eagle*, planted themselves on the surface of the Moon. I was sitting on my father's knee (having been wakened by my dad, much to the annoyance of my mother) when Armstrong uttered his famous, oft-misquoted sentence. Even at that tender age it was obvious to me that something very special had happened. It is one of those moments you never forget. I can only hope that my generation will see man land on both the Moon and Mars.

Revell, *Airfix* and *Monogram* all released models of the *Apollo* workhorse, the *Saturn V* launch vehicle, during the time of the *Apollo* missions. While *Revell* went for a scale of 1/96th, *Airfix* and *Monogram* chose the more shelf-friendly scale of 1/144th. Both 1/144th kits have their faults, but can be worked into a reasonable version with a bit of effort and by using parts from both kits.

Top to bottom, left to right: Layout of parts used for the build that were taken from the *Monogram* kit • The *Monogram* and *Airfix* *F1* parts side by side for comparison. The main fuel lines are attached to the *Monogram* parts, whereas the *Airfix* ones are separate • The Stage One mounting plate from both kits. The *F1* mounts from the *Airfix* parts will be cut out and used for the completed *F1* engines • A pair of completed *F1* engines. The *Airfix* mounts and fuel lines are very evident, other details coming from various kits • The finished *F1*s and new base plate cut from 80 thou *Plasticard*. Note the new detail scribed into the plate • With the fins attached, the tabs inside are removed and the interior filled and sanded • The ribbed truss detail is added • This photo shows the locking tabs for the First Stage (left) and removed (right). All the tabs were removed on all of the main parts.

63

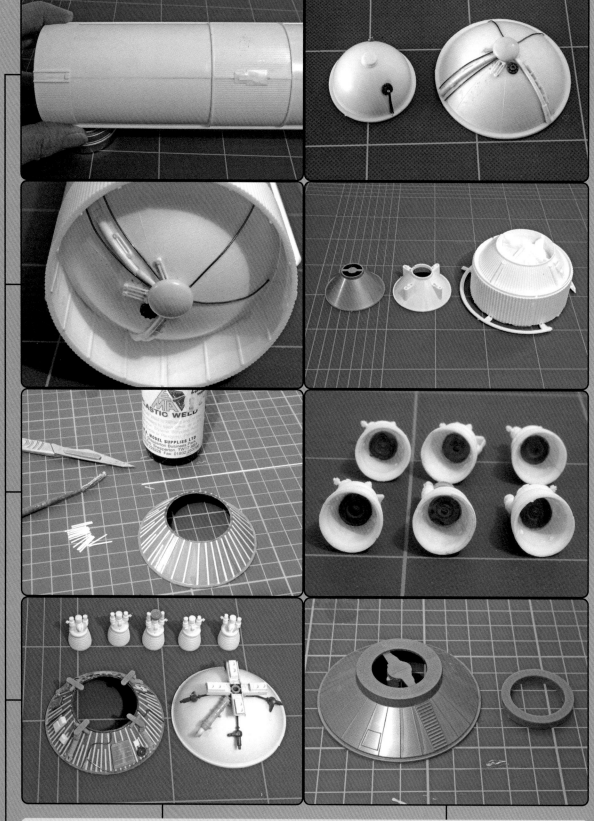

Top to bottom, left to right: Detail for the lifting points is added with *Plasticard* and strip • Fuel tanks for the First and Third Stages are detailed with a selection of wire and kit parts • The front of the First Stage showing the fuel tank in place and the internal ribs added to the inside edge with strip • This shot shows Second Stage engine mount parts from all the available commercial *Saturn V* kits (from left to right), *Monogram*, *Airfix* and *Revell* (1/96th). Only the *Revell* kit is even remotely accurate • With the *Monogram* parts cut down, new detail is added with plastic strip • The *Airfix* J2 engines have had detail added to cover the prominent mould pips • The detailed J2 engine mounts. The completed *Monogram* part, a new centre mount built atop of the *Airfix* fuel tank, and the J2 engines themselves • *Monogram*'s Second Stage lifting shroud as per the kit. An *EMA* ring will be used to replace the moulded top section, which is very basic.

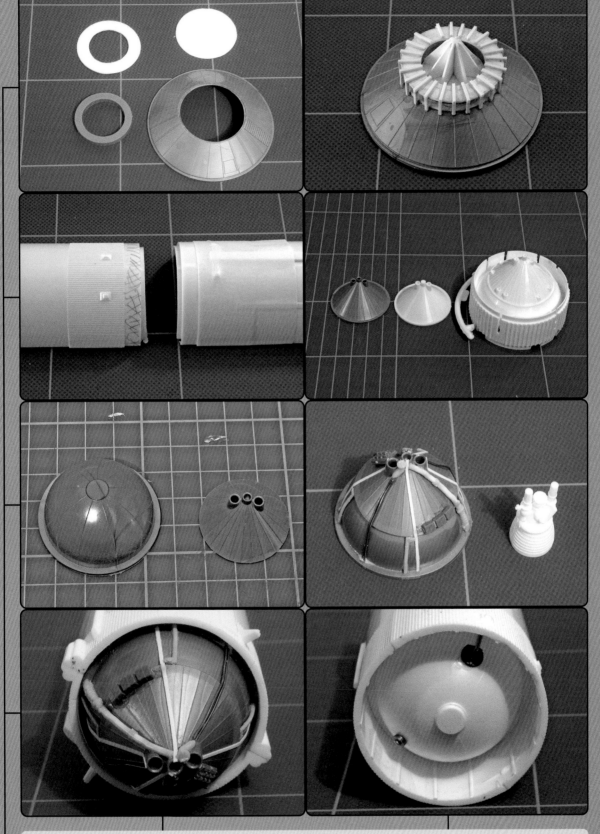

65

Top to bottom, left to right: The shroud has been cut down; a *Plasticard* base and ring have also been cut out • The completed shroud prior to clean up and painting. Although not dimensionally correct, it looks a whole lot better than the original part. 5mm must be removed from the top of the Third Stage • Another comparison shot, this time for the Third Stage J2 mount • The modified J2 mount (on right) about to be fitted to the Third Stage fuel tank • The completed 'new' Third Stage J2 engine mount • Again, strip, wire and kit parts have all been used • Test fitting the 'new' Third Stage mount • The front end of the Third Stage. The *Airfix* tank is used with minor extra detail (although the tank tip has been reduced, note the internal strip detail as per the First Stage).

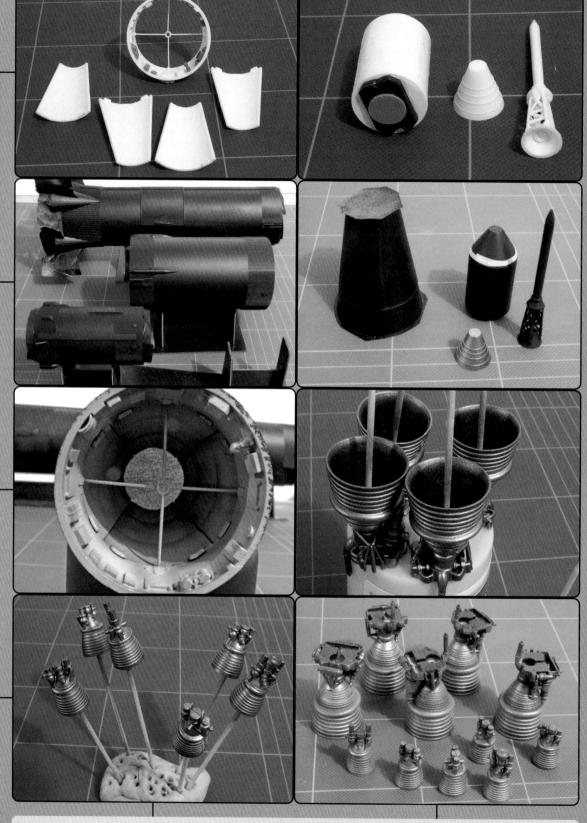

Top to bottom, left to right: The *Apollo* Spacecraft Adapter parts. These *Monogram* parts have been modified by removing their working mechanisms and adding detail to the base to represent the missing instrument ring • The remaining *Apollo* parts – note the new engine mount for the *CSM*, *Airfix* engine bell and modified *Escape Tower* • The First, Second and Third Stages being painted. All the internal surfaces have been painted and masked. The model parts are sitting on their specific custom-made display stands • The *Apollo* sub-assemblies primed and awaiting further colours. The Adapter has been built up at this stage • The inside of the built up Adapter – note the shading on the petals • The *F1* engines have received their base coat of metallic. The insides of the bells have been carefully misted to keep a sense of depth and scale • The *J2* engines with their base colour on. Cocktail sticks and *Blu-tak* are indispensable modelling tools! • In this shot both *F1* and *J2* engines have been carefully shaded with a copper/brown mix. Further shading with a dark wash will really bring them to life.

There are only three preserved *Saturn V*s currently on display – one of them at the *United States Space and Rocket Center* in Huntsville near the *Marshall Space Flight Center*, one at the *Kennedy Space Centre* in Florida (a mixture of various flight-ready and non flight-ready pieces, some originally built for future *Apollo* missions and mock-up parts), and the third at the *Lyndon B. Johnson Space Centre* in Houston, Texas. This is a complete, mission-ready *Saturn V*, made from components that were pulled from flight due to *NASA* cancellations. This mission-ready example is the only complete one of the three, although the Second Stage aft interstage and Third Stage aft interstage structure have been removed for better visitor access. Now restored and enclosed in its own purpose-built building, this is the version I have chosen to model, as it is displayed in real life on its side and split apart so that you can view the individual details of each stage.

The *Saturn V* launcher was designed and developed by a team under Dr. Wernher Von Braun at *NASA*'s *Marshall Space Flight Centre* specifically for the *Apollo* program. A total of fifteen were built, twelve being used for *Apollo* and one for the *Skylab* program. The remaining two were initially slated to be used as launch vehicles for the *Voyager* probes, but these would eventually be launched by *Titan Centaur*.

The best way to display this model is with the stages parted so you can see all the interior detail in each of them. For the 25th anniversary of the Moon landings I was commissioned to build a *Monogram* kit for a shop window display. I added various details here and there but, unfortunately, the client wanted the model to be capable of display both laying down and upright, which somewhat compromised its accuracy. Fifteen years later, when I was approached by the editor to contribute to this title, it seemed timely that I should build another, better version that was more representative of the full size rocket.

I used both *Airfix* and *Monogram* kits for the construction of this model – both kits are being reissued in 2009 for the 40th anniversary of the *Apollo 11* Moon landings (the *Airfix* version will contain a new sprue with ten new parts, that will – hopefully – address some of the more basic dimensional problems with this kit).

At no time did I decide to exactly copy every detail of the *Saturn V* in 1/144th. Instead the idea was to give an overall feel of the original without spending months building and assembling microscopic parts that no one (except for myself) would really appreciate. I also refuse to apologise for using a plethora of converted and non-converted commercial kit parts for some of these details, enabling me to build this model within publishing deadlines.

The Saturn V Launch Vehicle

First Stage S1C

The First Stage of the vehicle consumes a Kerosene and Liquid Oxygen mix, its five F1 engines pushing the vehicle to a height of 38 miles at a speed of 5,300 mph in two and a half minutes. The centre line F1 is static; the remaining four are gimballed to facilitate attitude control during flight. This stage was built by *Boeing* at *NASA*'s *Michoud Assembly Facility* (MAF) in New Orleans. The First Stage displayed at *JSC* was originally scheduled for the cancelled *Apollo 19*.

The main parts of the First Stage came from the *Monogram* kit. This is because the *Airfix* kit's First Stage detail is quite heavy, the *Monogram* parts looking better. Construction started with the F1 engines. These were chosen over the *Airfix* examples as the insides of the bells could be filled and smoothed out, whereas the *Airfix* bells have very prominent alignment pins that are extremely difficult to deal with. The *Monogram* fuel lines were removed and (once the damage had been dealt with) replaced with ones cut from the *Airfix* parts. The mounts were cut from the *Airfix* First Stage engine base and carefully fettled down, detailing being added before a new base was shaped from 80thou *Plasticard* and scribed with a more authentic pattern, the *Monogram* base being retained as a pattern for placement during final construction. The fins were attached to the bottom of the First Stage. Inside the bottom part the fin tabs were then trimmed down, with any protruding mould pips being removed and sanded smooth. Although *JSC*'s *Saturn V* has

Top to bottom, left to right: Here the fuel tanks, Second Stage lifting shroud and Third Stage engine mount have been given their basic colour coats • And here are the finished items. Every trick in my armoury was used to make these look as realistic as possible in such a small scale • The basic colours on the *Apollo* spacecraft have been added • With the basic colours on and the masking removed on the main stage parts decals are added, mostly from the *Airfix* kit. Their quality provoked language not suitable for a publication such as this! • The Second Stage *J2* mounts, painted, weathered and awaiting final assembly • The new First Stage *F1* engine base was detailed with different shades of grey and rivets added with a *Faber and Castell* fine-tipped pen. Further coats of white tinted varnish would tone down the effect to a better scale appearance • Locking pins are being added to the leading edge of the Third Stage with the aforementioned *Faber and Castell* pen. The edge has been hand-painted with *Humbrol* Trainer Yellow that had been toned down with a little tan • *Plasti-kote*'s *Fast Dry* enamel spray. This amazing product was used for the Helium tanks around the third stage *J2* mount. Sprayed over matt black it gives amazing results.

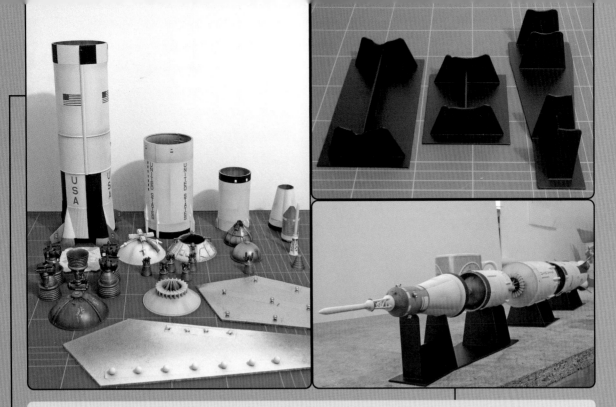

Above left: All the component parts laid out ready for final assembly. Note the *EMA* acrylic spheres used for J2 and Third Stage Helium tanks. Top right: The display stands finished in a tough automotive matt black spray. Above right: The finished model sitting on my bench ready for its photo shoot.

had two of its fins and fairings removed to allow the rocket to sit lower and therefore afford a better view, I decided that my finished model would look better with a complete First Stage. Rod bracing was also added inside the fairing – not as complex as that on the real *Saturn V*, but enough to give an impression.

The main halves' locking tabs for the Second Stage aft intersection were cut off (all the tabs were removed from all the parts as they are not needed). Plastic strip detail was applied to the inside and the halves were glued together with the base part also added. Further detail was then glued to the outside of the completed part, this comprising of lifting points and raised strips around the middle ribbed section, which looks far better and more authentic than the existing detail. Detailing was also then added to the *Airfix* fuel tank part, completing construction of the First Stage. I decided not to build the original lifting cage as fitted to the *JSC* version because, although it would be accurate, I felt it would have made for a less interesting model as the tank detail would have been difficult to see.

Second Stage S2

The Second Stage burns a mixture of Liquid Hydrogen and Liquid Oxygen, boosting the vehicle to a height of 114 miles in 6 minutes. It is powered by five J2 engines that are arranged and gimballed in exactly the same way as the First Stage. This stage was built by *North American Rockwell's Space Division* at Seal Beach, California. The Second Stage at *JSC* was scheduled for *Apollo 20*.

With the exception of the J2 engines and a fuel tank, which came from the *Airfix* kit, the majority of the Second Stage came from the *Monogram* parts as the *Airfix* Second Stage features some very odd detailing. It is also moulded with the aft interstage structure from the Third Stage attached to it, whereas the *Monogram* parts present this as a separate item.

Both kits woefully lack any kind of realistic detail for the J2 engine mounts. The lifting shroud is only catered for by *Monogram* but requires a lot of work in order to make it look authentic.

Above: Rear shot of the completed model (low angle). Opposite page: Third Stage and *Apollo* Spacecraft rear perspective shot.

Work starts with the engine mounts. A gimballed mount was constructed on top of the *Airfix* fuel tank and fuel line detail was added, the *Monogram* part then being cut down and rib detail applied to it using strip. Further detailing was created using modified kit parts, various thicknesses of strip and metal wire. The J2 engines were built up and a rear bulkhead included inside the bell and the moulded part numbers removed (*EMA* acrylic spheres were added to the J2 engine following painting, giving a much needed authenticity).

The lifting shroud was modified by removing the top section and replacing it with one constructed from *Plasticard* and strip around an *EMA* ring.

The locking mechanisms were removed from each end of the stage halves and the ullage rockets carefully drilled out. The Second Stage halves were then glued together, completing Second Stage construction.

Third Stage S4B

Stage Three is powered by a single, gimballed J2 engine. However, unlike the previous stages it can be switched off and restarted. Its first burn is for two and a half minutes, which accelerates the vehicle to 17,400 mph, a stable orbital velocity. Following this orbit (usually one only to achieve position for Lunar Trajectory), the engine is fired again for five minutes, pushing the vehicle to 24,400 mph, which is Earth Gravity escape velocity. *McDonnell Douglas Astronautics Co.* at Huntington Beach, California built the Third Stage. *Disc*'s Third Stage was scheduled for *Apollo 18*.

The first thing that strikes you about both the *Monogram* and *Airfix* parts is that they are approximately six scale feet too long. This is because the instrument ring is moulded on top of the Third Stage instead of being separate. The instrument ring is attached to the *Apollo Spacecraft* on the JSC display.

After removing the locking mechanisms from the *Monogram* stage halves, 5mm was removed from the top of the parts before they were cemented together and the remainder of the kit detail added. Rib detail was applied to the top inside edge before moving on to the J2 mount. Both kits cater for this pretty well, despite their depicting it as a constant angle, whereas in reality it is a cone sitting atop a hemisphere.

The *Monogram* parts were used for the mount. I first removed the top section of the standard part then attached this to what should have been the fuel tank. Detail was then applied using strip, kit parts and wire. The *Airfix* tank part replaced the

Monogram version, to which I added a small amount of detail and sanded the top pip back somewhat as this is not as prominent on the full-size version.

A single J2 engine was built using the *Airfix* parts to maintain continuity, as the *Monogram* J2 has a very deep bell and would have looked odd against the *Airfix* J2s on the Second Stage.

EMA spheres of a smaller diameter than the ones used for the J2 engines were added to represent the Helium repressurisation spheres again, once painting was complete.

The Apollo Spacecraft

This Stands 25m tall and consists of the *Lunar Module, Spacecraft Lunar Module Adapter, Service Module, Command Module Boost Protective Cover* and *Launch Escape System.*

JSC's *Apollo Spacecraft* is missing its *LEM*, the remainder of the *Apollo* spacecraft on display being from a cancelled flight on the *Skylab* program (the *Saturn 1b* launch vehicle shares its Third Stage with the *Saturn V* and is therefore compatible with *Apollo* spacecraft). The *Service* and *Command Modules* were built by *North American Rockwell* along with *Sc2* at their Seal Beach facility in California. The *Lunar Modules* were built by *Grumman.*

JSC's *Saturn V* does not have a *LEM* on display, only the *CSM* and *CM*. In fact, the entire *Apollo Spacecraft* is displayed (minus the *LEM*) as a single section.

The Module Adapter was the trickiest part of the entire build and was built using *Monogram* parts. I applied a small amount of kit-bashed and strip detailing to the inside of the base part to represent the instrument ring. The bracing structure was made from a kit part and plastic rod was added to the top of the part (this brace is in place on the *JSC* display to give strength to the structure while on display, as the original *LEM* stand is not present). The adapter petals then had their mould pips and locking mechanisms removed. These parts were then painted and weathered before being built up into the complete Adapter and masked ready for main painting.

The *CSM* was next, this being constructed from *Monogram* parts, although the manoeuvring thrusters came from the *Airfix* kit, after the original *Monogram* moulded-on versions had been removed with a sharp scalpel, together with the main engine bell. A new, more accurate engine bell mount was modified from a 1/35th *Sherman* tank kit part.

The *Escape Tower* was a mixture of *Monogram* and *Airfix* parts. The *CM* shroud (*Monogram*) was cut down, as the *JSC* shroud has been removed to protect the *CM* as it was in a bad state of decay (the moisture generated by outside weather conditions between the shroud and the *CM* was, quite literally, rusting it away). The *Airfix* Tower halves were then glued together and the lattice was very carefully scraped with the tip of a scalpel blade to give a better scale appearance. They were then attached to the cut down shroud and escape rockets were added, these being

thruster parts from an *Airfix* 1/72nd *Lunar Module*.

There now followed a great deal of very careful filling and sanding to all the component parts in readiness for painting.

I next built the stands from 80 thou *Plasticard*. The full size *Saturn V* sections sit on bright blue lattice cradles. However, time constraints restricted me to building more simplified versions. I also wanted my First Stage to be complete, whereas the *JSC* version is missing its lower fairings and tail fins.

Painting

A subject such as the *Saturn V* is always a difficult one to finish correctly – painting should be subtle, to impact a sense of scale and colour, and applied very carefully.

Above and below: Second Stage rear and front perspective shots.

I primed all the parts in acrylic matt black from an automotive spray can. The main markings were then masked off on all the stages and all the internal colours applied. These were a mixture of subtle and not so subtle custom metallic shades mixed from the *Liquitex* range, highlights and lowlights being airbrushed with *Vallejo* custom grey mixes.

Once the *Lunar Module* Adapter had been built up and the ends of each stage masked off, matt white was carefully misted over all the parts, building up the density slowly over many passes. The masking was removed, the parts were sealed with *Johnsons Klear/Future* and the decals added. Unfortunately, my *Monogram* versions were yellowed and fractured beyond use, so these came from the *Airfix* sheets. I say *sheets* as the printing was so poor that I ended up scraping together just enough from three separate sheets! The decals, in turn, were sealed with further coats of *Klear*.

The F1, J2 and *CM* engine bells were sprayed with alternate passes of *Liquitex* silver and rich silver, which gave them a very authentic look. The F1 and J2s were then aged with a wash mixture of *Vallejo* black and black grey with a touch of dark green and a rust mix of copper with field drab.

The First Stage fuel tank was sprayed a custom metallic grey before being weathered with various mixes of *Vallejo* paints including orange, flat earth and black grey. I treated the grey with liquid mask, rubbing off certain areas as I applied each coat of colour.

The Second Stage lifting shroud was painted in trainer yellow and shaded with turner yellow, the *Vallejo* dark wash mixture being applied around the top of the shroud only. The J2 mounts were misted in matt white, various details being picked out with *Vallejo* paints with a brush and a steady hand. These parts were then carefully weathered with the dark wash and matt varnish tinted with white.

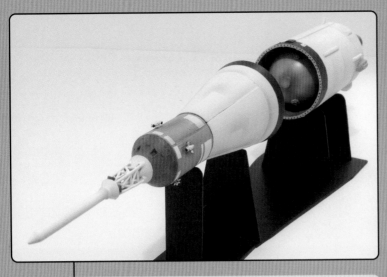

The J2 mount for the Third Stage was painted in a combination of custom-mixed metallic shades, *Testors* brass being used for the gold areas and the fuel tank being a custom-mixed metallic grey. Both parts were aged with the *Vallejo* dark wash.

The *Command Module* was painted field drab. Light grey and flat brown were added with a brush before being misted with *Floquil* rust. The *Service Module* was painted with another custom metallic mix.

Finally, the First Stage base was painted white and various panels picked out in two shades of grey. Rivets were applied with a *Castell & Faber* fine-tipped pen and the whole effect deadened with many coats of white-tinted matt varnish.

Above: Third Stage and *Apollo* Spacecraft front perspective shot.
Below: First Stage rear perspective shot.

The main body parts were given a coat of matt varnish and shaded with a subtle mixture of white grey. The rims of the stages were painted trainer yellow (dulled with a small dab of tan) and the locking points picked out again with a *Castell & Faber* pen.

The *EMA* spheres were sprayed matt black then coated with matt white (for the larger ones) and *Plasti-kote*'s chrome for the Helium tanks on the Third Stage. This chrome paint is the best on the market, giving a really good effect. Other colours such as brass, copper and gold are also available.

Finally, the stands had all their edges sanded smooth and sprayed matt black. All the components for the model were then glued together using superglue. This took a fair amount of time as I hadn't quite taken 'paint thickness' into account, so careful sanding was needed to achieve a good fit of parts. Once this was completed, the model sections were placed on their stands.

The finished model certainly has the wow factor and makes an excellent addition to any Real Space collection. Although it took many more hours than I originally thought it would, I'm pleased with the finished article.

The original mission statement for project *Apollo* was to explore the moon and then go on to Mars using updated *Saturn V* and *Nova* launch vehicles. Unfortunately none of this came to pass, although *NASA* intends to return to the Moon in 2014. Until that time, the *Saturn V* at *Lyndon B. Johnston Space Centre* stands as a reminder that, one summer's day in 1969, the people of the Earth really did come together as one. We can only hope that future *NASA* missions can rekindle that kind of optimism and hope.

'They came in peace for all Mankind'.

Moon Modeller!

A look at the intricate **Real Space** projects of **Pete Malaguti**

Real Space modeller Pete Malaguti has always been fascinated with, and indeed has worked in, the Aerospace industry. His main interest, however, is the American Space Program, a fascination that began when he was a child. 'I was actually around for the first *Mercury* flights and vividly recall the first manned Moon Landing,' he notes. Despite this almost lifelong passion, however, his first accurised Real Space model was only completed recently, in November, 2006.

As a boy Pete made all the space kits available at the time, most of them coming together in an afternoon. Today he'll spend up to two hundred hours building just one of these subjects. Since that first build in 2006 Pete feels he's learned so much more about *Mercury*, *Gemini* and *Apollo* than he ever knew before. 'The fun of it lies in the challenge of trying to replicate these complex vehicles as accurately as possible.'

In the following article we showcase some of Pete's exacting Real Space modelling projects, each being accompanied by his own notes detailing how he accomplished the builds.

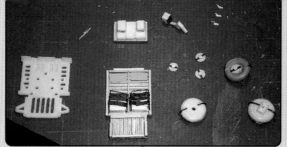

Above: *Apollo 16* Ascent Stage modifications; *LRV* parts; Q-tip sections added to landing gear.
Below and opposite: two views of the completed *Apollo 16* miniature.

Apollo 16

This is the old 1/72 *Airfix Lunar Module*. It's quite inaccurate, so to accurise it I looked at an old (1972) article on Sven Knudsen's modeller's site, specifically pertaining to making this kit accurate. That, plus numerous photographs on the *Apollo Lunar Surface Journal* site helped me out.

I first beefed up the secondary landing gear struts with segments from cotton swabs. Then, on the Ascent Stage, I enlarged the two triangular windows and created the small rendezvous window on top. I cut out the front door and built a new one with sheet styrene. The left and right side panels on the Ascent Stage needed to be completely rebuilt as well. The new panels were made from sheet styrene and thin aluminium sheet. The long handrail, between the windows, was made from piano wire. The vent hoods were installed and the four thruster housings were narrowed.

The Descent Stage had the panel removed where the LRV was stored. The other sections, or 'Quads', were built up to more accurately show certain details. The RTG cask was scratchbuilt, as well as the landing radar and its shield. The Descent Stage was covered in a couple of different shades of gold foil, plus normal household aluminium foil (on the bottom) and foil painted a tint of gunmetal. The plume deflectors were also scratchbuilt using copper wire for the supports and aluminium sheet for the deflectors themselves.

In the *Rover* Quad I placed aluminium disks, stamped out using a Waldron punch, representing pulleys and other hardware inside the bay. The front porch was narrowed and thinned and I replaced the handrails with bent copper wire.

All five antennae were rebuilt too, as the kit-supplied ones were way off. I used plastic rod, aluminium tube and rod and piano wire to rebuild them.

The *Lunar Rover* was scratchbuilt, except for the wheels. I used the *Airfix* 1/72 Astronaut 'kit', in which were two sets of *Rover* wheels, but they are polyethylene and, as I quickly learned, nothing sticks to them. I coated them with *Future Floor Wax* and used a variety of glues. The parts hold, but they are very tenuous and delicate. The LRV floor pan was built from styrene pieces and I included the folded down seats, console, handrails, foot pads, *Velcro* straps and the four pegs attached to the frame, not to mention the suspension parts.

The astronauts experienced some surgery too. I removed and repositioned arms and legs and scraped some material from the helmets' visor areas to represent a more accurate profile. Some small pieces of aluminium foil were used to create flaps on their PLSS backpacks.

Quite a few more additions/corrections were also made to this *LM*.

Apollo 15 Rover

This *Apollo 15 Lunar Module* is the 1/48 scale *Revell/Monogram* kit. The *Rover* was the first completely scratchbuilt model I'd ever made (taking 37 hours to complete) and the *LM* features a great many modifications (over 200 hours to complete). The four Quads have been cut out to show the different equipment bays. Quad 1, to the viewer's right of the ladder, had the *Rover*; Quad 2 the ALSEP package and the RTG cask (the access doors on this Quad actually open in an 'accordion' mode, like the real thing); Quad 3, the *Rover* equipment pallets and Quad 4 the extended stay MESA.

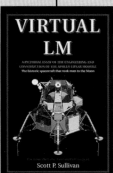

VIRTUAL
LM

A PICTORIAL ESSAY OF THE ENGINEERING AND
CONSTRUCTION OF THE APOLLO LUNAR MODULE
The historic spacecraft that took man to the Moon

Scott P. Sullivan

There are over 30 scratchbuilt modifications to this model. For instance, all 5 antennae have been rebuilt. The ladder has been rebuilt and I've included the hook for weighing the lunar rock samples. The porch was rebuilt and I attached a handle on either side of it, one for the MESA deployment and the other for the *Rover* deployment. The Descent Stage was covered in three different colours of foil. The gold colours are from chocolate bars sold here in Canada (*Aero* and *Caramilk*). The black foil was a tint of flat black painted on household aluminium foil and adhered with *Microscale Foil Adhesive*. The landing gear probes were installed and bent up. Thin gold tape was placed all over the *LM* where applicable, as per my photo references. The MESA was detailed and the electrometric strap included. Vent hoods were placed on the Ascent Stage, the RCS thrusters were hollowed out, the landing radar and its protective shield were rebuilt and much, much, *much* more.

The panels on the Ascent Stage were cut out of thin, 7 thou, printer plate aluminium sheet and bent to conform to the kit. The panels were glued with CA glue. The panels on the rear of the Ascent Stage were bent to simulate the loads and forces endured upon landing. The rendezvous window was cut out. Little details were included, like the umbilical connection on the Ascent Stage and the SLA umbilical connectors on the Descent Stage. I used Rick Sternbach's excellent decals and windows for the model. I also extensively used Scott P. Sullivan's superb reference book, *Virtual LM*. It was absolutely indispensable. Any detail I needed was included in his book. I also want to thank Paul Fjeld for his advice on the placement of the electrometric strap which 'extends' the MESA.

This spread: *Apollo 15* diorama complete with *Lunar Rover Vehicle* (*LRV*). Inset: Scott P. Sullivan's reference book, *Virtual LM*.

I also detailed the astronauts (I made four of 'em). I cut apart the arms and legs and re-attached them to depict the famous *Apollo 15* photo with Jim Irwin, the *LM* and the *Rover*. Homemade decals, antennae, sample bags (made from bent aluminium from a frozen lasagne pan lid) and attaching straps (household aluminium foil painted off-white), were glued to the astronauts' backpacks (PLSS). Dirt on their suits was simulated with a light spray of grey paint. The visors were painted and seven coats of *Future*, with yellow food colouring, were used to give a nice, tinted, glossy look to the visors. The astronaut depicting Dave Scott (with red stripes) has a scratchbuilt camera attached to his chest. The lunar base was also scratchbuilt using a piece of drywall as the base and large amounts of 'spackle' spread over it as a base from which to make all the craters. Footprints were created using a tiny, scratchbuilt footpad with grooves.

The *Rover* is a separate story. It has over 230 parts, home made decals, removable tools and an operating hinged equipment pallet on the back.

Apollo 12 with Surveyor

The LM model is the *Monogram* 1/48 scale kit. This model took around 150 hours to complete and is built to depict *Apollo 12*'s pinpoint landing on the moon, just 600 ft. from the unmanned *Surveyor* spacecraft in November, 1969.

I used *New Ware* aftermarket items including: plume deflectors, landing radar and its shield, flag carrier on ladder, front porch, handles on either side of it for MESA deployment, vent hoods on Ascent Stage, four antennae on Ascent Stage, headlight and docking lights on *LM* 'face', rendezvous window cut out, docking target, reaction control system (RCS), thruster nozzles… and more.

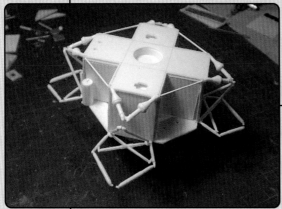
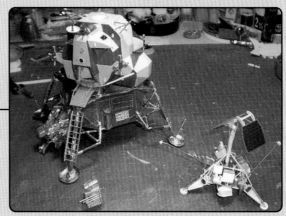

I made over 20 modifications to the LM, including:
- Scratchbuilding of all 4 Quads.
- (RTG) Radioisotopic Thermoelectric Generator assembly was scratchbuilt.
- Quad 4 – scratchbuilt MESA with insulating blankets and electrometric strap, used to deploy the MESA.
- Lunar surface sensing probes on three landing gear legs.
- Three different coloured foils on Descent Stage. The foil was household aluminium foil painted dark grey and foil from two different chocolate bars sold here in Canada. It was adhered using *Microscale Micro Metal Foil Adhesive*.
- Gold Tape on Ascent and Descent Stages to cover seams on foil, just like the real thing.
- Aluminium tube on secondary landing struts.
- Rebuilt ladder.
- Optical telescope hood behind front rendezvous antenna.

The *Surveyor* was completely scratchbuilt using styrene, aluminium and brass rod adhered with CA glue.

I used Rick Sternbach's (*Space Model Systems*) superb decals and windows. Once again I referred to Scott Sullivan's amazing reference book, *Virtual LM*.

Apollo 17 Rover
This is the 1/32 *EVA Models Lunar Rover* and my first all-resin kit. Chris Chulamanis, who passed away just after New Year's 2008, did an outstanding job on this kit. No air bubbles, easy-to-understand, well-illustrated instructions and very well thought out. I scratchbuilt the aft equipment pallet to depict *Apollo 17*. The diorama shows the astronauts' visit to the Taurus-Littrow site, *Station 6*, in December, 1972. The *Apollo 17* landing site, named for the Taurus mountains and Littrow crater, is located in a

This spread: *Apollo 12 LEM* and *Surveyor* diorama.

mountainous region on the southeastern rim of the Mare Serenitatis basin. I initially used the figures from the kit, one standing, one seated, but decided, after watching the *Spacecraft Film* on *Apollo 17*, to have the Gene Cernan figure walking from the LRV to the 'Jack' Schmitt figure. I contacted Chris at *EVA* and he obliged me by sending me another standing figure. I then modified each figure by repositioning arms and legs and shaving material from the visor area of the helmets to more accurately represent them. You may notice I've also added straps and hoses to the astronaut figures as well as tongs and a hammer to the Cernan figure (red stripes). I then scratchbuilt the equipment pallet to show the version of the LRV used on *Apollo 17*, using styrene, some aluminium sheet (from a commercial printer), styrene rods and 1/16" aluminium tube. The LRV has seat belts, a map holder, a tool attached to the mast and a few other customised items on it. The LRV and astronaut figures were then sprayed with a couple of shades of grey to represent lunar dust, which went everywhere. The 'lunar' base is *masonite* (I also used foam rubber to create the slope and the big boulders) with crack filler (spackle) spread over it. You may also see the scratchbuilt Gnomon by the Schmitt figure. One of its uses was to get accurate colours when printing the photos. The website, *Apollo Lunar Surface Journal*, was my prime photographic reference tool. Just about every photo taken on an *Apollo* lunar mission is on that site. This is a very good kit. Well cast resin, photo-etch parts and excellent instructions made this a fun build.

Revell 1/24 Gemini

The kit fits together really poorly and I think the original moulds from the 1960s were used, so I've had to do a lot of scratchbuilding. This particular model depicts the flight of *Gemini 9A*, in 1966, with Gene Cernan performing his spacewalk. I scratchbuilt the ejection seats, the hatch interiors, the capsule interior, the aft adapters and the AMU (Astronaut Manoeuvring Unit) which astronaut Cernan was supposed to use to fly around the spacecraft. I even rebuilt the Cernan figure out of *Tamiya Epoxy Putty*, using only the kit's head and torso. The aft adapter sections were accurised with the addition of access panels and more surface detail. In addition, the *Update* kit, including new resin thrusters for the adapter section, was from Glenn Johnson at *Real Space Models* and the decals from Rick Sternbach at *Space Model Systems*. The black spots on the adapter section depict *Velcro* patches, which were used to assist Cernan in moving around back there.

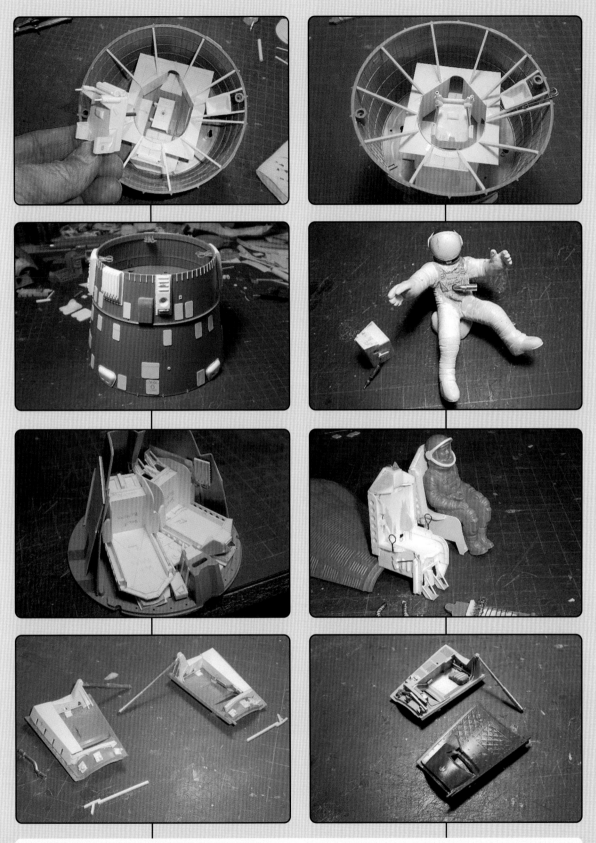

Opposite page: *Apollo 17 Lunar Rover Vehicle.*

Top to bottom: *Gemini 9A capsule*—aft end AMU with pin; aft with tether guide; access doors on adaptor; astronaut with ELSS; cockpit—assembly dry run; seats, hoses and ceiling panel; preliminary work on hatches; hatches (before and after).

He also had *Velcro* patches on his palms. The gold 'curtain' protecting the equipment in the aft section was made from a grocery bag, cut into sections and adhered with rubber cement. It's still holding well! This was a lot of fun to build and took about 120 hours to complete. In researching this mission I learned a heckova lot about the *Gemini* program as well as this specific mission. The *Gemini* CD from *Spacecraft Films* was a huge help in accurising the hardware.

Cutaway LM

This model is based on the *Monogram* 1/48 *LM*. I replaced most of the kit parts and the figure – there's only about 15% of the original kit remaining. I was initially going to just cut away part of the starboard side of the Ascent Stage, but the more I researched it, the more I decided to remove. My main reference was the CD included in the book *Virtual LM*. I used the images on the CD as well as a wide variety of engineering drawings from a variety of online sources.

I started by building the basic frame of the Ascent Stage and scaling all the various bits and pieces to replicate the fuel and oxidiser tanks, wiring and equipment. Then I built the stringers on the front section, referring to lots of photos. For the windows I used *Space Model Systems* windows and the *New Ware* (aftermarket) resin and photo-etch goodies for EVA handrails, thruster nozzles, docking tunnel and more. Aluminium printer plate was used to replicate the cutaway portion of the Ascent Stage.

The Descent Stage began by cutting off the panels from the octagonal kit part. The top of the Descent Stage was modified to show the large fuel tanks peeking through the top. The removed panels were then scratchbuilt by scribing structural lines and gluing strips of styrene to replicate the structural elements. The wiring is copper wire. The landing pads are from *New Ware* and two of the landing struts were built from aluminium tube... and they operate. *New Ware* photo-etch parts are visible all over the landing gear. Chocolate bar wrappers were used to cover the Descent Stage.

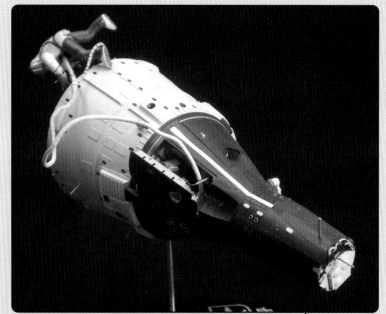

Top and above: *Gemini 9A* capsule.

Opposite: *LM* cutaway—front section stringers are assembled; front section with RCS mount; CA-cabling; Ascension Stage viewed aft; CA struts assembled; Ascension and Descent Stages viewed from rear left.

Opposite bottom: completed *LM* cutaway viewed from Quadrant three.

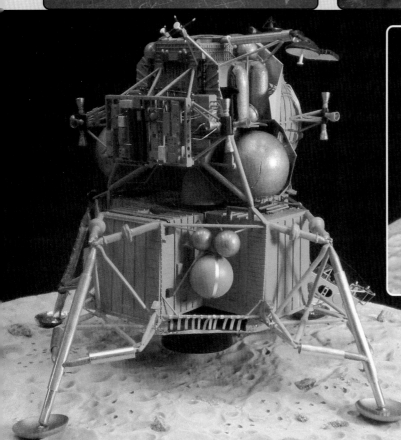

Improving Airfix's Classic Lunar Module

Article and photographs by Mike Adamson

When *Airfix* originally released their *Lunar Module* in 1:72nd scale it was eagerly built by a generation of starry-eyed kids entranced by the reality of *Project Apollo*. To this day the decal sheet offers placards for the first moon landing, which is dated, and the second, which is not, as if *Apollo 12* had not yet flown when the kit was issued in, presumably, late 1969. The larger *Monogram* kit was more costly, and today the original *Airfix* issue has the benefit of being perhaps more readily available*, despite the demise and resurrection of the company some two years ago (*Airfix* has so far been through about half as many business reincarnations as *Doctor Who*, another British institution impervious to time!)

As with any classic-era kit, it has a good many issues – not just issues with fit or flash, as are endemic to kits of the '60s and '70s, but the underlying issues of accuracy and faithfulness to the details of the original subject. It was common practice at the time to

*Airfix have just re-released a 40th. Anniversary edition of this subject – see page 5 – Ed.

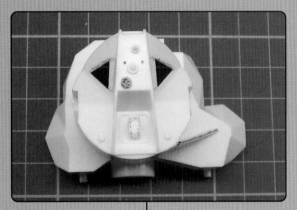

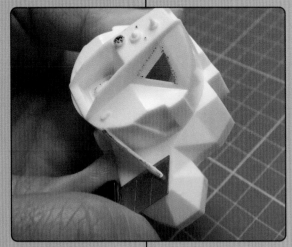

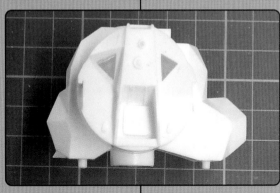

sacrifice detail accuracy in the interests of simplicity of moulding, and, to be fair, only with the advent of modern slide-mould technology has this limitation in kit-making been seriously tackled, and then only for subjects with a proven marketplace for an expensive final product.

Airfix's kit is simple, with only 25 parts for the lower stage and 47 for the upper, some of them being pretty small… a moderate count but plenty for younger hobbyists of the time to tackle with minimal tools and stringy tube glue. While the outline is generally correct there are all sorts of detail issues to challenge the experienced modeller looking to build a serious replica from this kit. Some of them are worth tackling whilst others, unfortunately, just aren't.

Research

Photography is an excellent source for details, at once both enlightening and frustrating. There are exceptional photographs out there in printed literature and on the Web, but many of the cherry shots are those taken in space, and the harsh lighting conditions make visual analysis difficult by obliterating some details in glare and others in inky shadow. It also quickly becomes apparent that the *LM* for each flight was subtly different from its stable-mates, as was true for all elements of hardware for the *Apollo Program*, which were subject to continuous upgrade between flights to improve performance and utility. The big picture was essentially unchanged, however, and it falls to the modeller to decide if he or she is reproducing a specific *LM* or aiming to create a 'generic *LM*' with a detail suite most often seen in the best photographs. The former would call for exceptional depth of research but the information is probably out there. The latter can be tackled with more general source material.

A factor which emerges from the research is that pretty much the whole of the spacecraft's surface was covered with insulative material – metal foil on the Descent Stage but also something non-reflective cladding the Ascent Stage, secured panel by panel. This is another factor to consider in the depth to which the detailing is to be taken. Also, what colour were these materials? They appear grey or a khaki-buff depending on lighting angle, and seem different from picture to picture, which suggests either genuine difference between spacecraft or a luminosity factor in the surface finish creating difference due to lighting conditions. The model is obliged to be one fixed value and will never be seen in light as harsh as all the best photographs were taken in, so an approximation is the best bet.

Accuracy is also a wide open question, given to a very loose interpretation by many sources out there. A quick Web search on '*Lunar Module* models' turns up a huge

Top to bottom: Figs 1, 2, 3a and 3b.

number of replicas on offer from a great many sources. They all look different, none of them looks particularly like the real spacecraft in photographs, many are clearly out of proportion, and some are, bluntly put, toy-like junk at exorbitant prices, excused by the term 'collectable'. Therefore any reasonably accurate replica is going to stack up well by the standards of scale modelling.

I first built the *Airfix LM* when I was a teenager, and dutifully finished it in *Humbrol* flat white, flat black and chrome silver, applied thickly with a brush. We tend to trust the authority of the issuing company at that age, and follow their instructions willingly; it never occurs to us to really question how truthful-to-subject their product is; and what research sources would be available to us to crosscheck, anyway? In the age of the Internet we have no such excuse, and there are many excellent books out there, so we can at least get a bit closer to the real thing with minimal perspiration. Perhaps the best modeller's reference produced to date is the *Space in Miniature* volume (SIM #7) *Apollo Lunar Module*, detailing all nine flight vehicles from a modeller's perspective. You can find it here: http://www.spaceinminiature.com/books/sim7.html

Assessing the Model

The first thing to grasp is that no two parts are actually the same, meaning they don't actually fit. Take the thruster quad mounts as an example – each is a two-part assembly which sits back into a cutaway on the Ascent Stage. The parts need considerable cleanup once joined, and the cutaways are a different size to the sub-assemblies, requiring shims and/or filler (Fig. 4 shows what I mean by this). The kit is a simple one conceptually, but takes work to get up to speed (imagine if *FineMolds* or *Tamiya* gave us a *Lunar Module* in 1:24th scale. It would do everything but fly round the room).

An examination of the kit parts shows that *Airfix* simplified many details. There is a stiffening beam stretching between the lower left of the cockpit front out to the housing of the fuel tank to port, and this was cast not as a strut but as a solid sheet. This must be carved away and replaced with a rod. The struts supporting the RCS quad blast shields are totally absent (the shields are attached to the thrusters), so you have the option of building these. The characteristic gold foil insulation of the Descent Stage was omitted as probably being impossible to mould, and this is the biggest job facing the detailer.

The triangular windows flanking the hatch appeared too small but, after checking better photographs, I decided they were appreciably correct. However, they are at an angle to the edges of the panel into which they are set (they should be parallel) and the clear parts were marred by sink-marks on their outer faces, so I had at least some corrective surgery to do there. A bulge exists

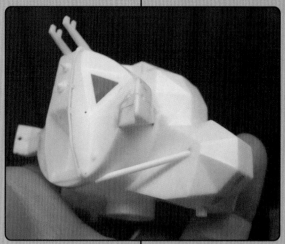

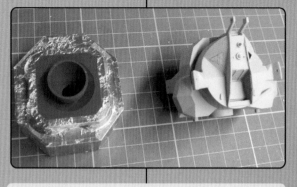

Top to bottom: Figs 4, 5, 6a and 6b.

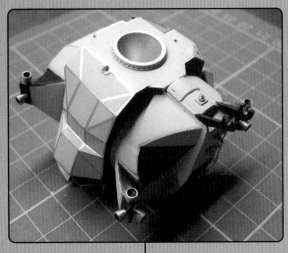

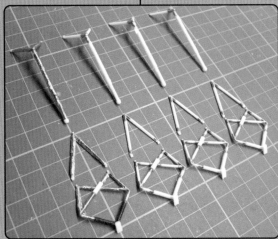

in the middle of the hatch which doesn't seem to match the visible details of any *LM* in any photo I have found so far, not even the box art, so this, too, would need to be corrected. Some of the antennae and instruments on the upper central panel above the hatch did not especially match photographs, so these would be carved away and adjusted also. These modifications are marked in black pen on the kit part in Fig. 1.

Airfix moulded the Descent Stage with a flare-out: it's wider at the bottom by 1mm+ over the top. Is this detail correct? If so, it's hard to see on the real spacecraft. There is an almost-profile photo of *Apollo 9*'s *LM Spider* in orbit over the Earth and, though proportion is difficult to assess due to shadows, it *seems* that the flare *is* present. It would be a peculiar detail for *Airfix* to invent! The geometry of the landing legs is also set up to match this flare and, as this is supposed to be an exercise in kit detailing, not scratchbuilding, I decided to accept this detail at face value.

Ascent Stage

My decision was to build a generic *LM* featuring the suite of details most commonly seen in photographs. Research ultimately pointed me in the general direction of *Apollo 14*'s *Antares*, as this craft was in some of my most representational images (though a few details from *Intrepid* and *Challenger* are probably there too).

I started with the Ascent Stage. Modifications focussed on the 'face' of the machine, those eye-windows and mouth-hatch, the instruments at the brow, and that cheekbone out to the ear-fuel tank. The strut that was moulded as a sheet was cut away completely with a knife (Fig. 2), and the attachment points adzed, filed and sanded flush. As that unidentified structure on the hatch is within the hatch void it's impossible to get a tool to it, so I cut the hatch away completely from the back.

The windows I decided to leave be as far as their proportions went, but those sink-marks in the plastic needed remedying. I used *Testor Clear Parts Cement*, applied with the rounded end of a fine paintbrush over the whole area of each window with the parts still on the sprue, to fill the concavities and find its level across the area as a continuous film which would (hopefully) dry crystal clear. It took a while to dry fully as the central area was quite thick. After five or six applications the sink marks were just about invisible, and the same cement was used to attach the parts from the back. I could perhaps have requested replacement parts from *Airfix*'s after sales office, but the likelihood of getting un-dimpled parts was, I felt, remote. It may be the age of the moulds, but sink holes are rife on other parts too.

The hatch was simply replaced with a piece of .020" plasticard, 8mm x 8mm, to reproduce the flat hatch seen in pictures, seated onto the raised lip which neatly recreates the appearance of the hatch standing away from the surrounding surface. Two structural details were added to the slope above the hatch in .010" x .020" strip. Two details removed from the 'brow' area were replaced with slivers of .020" round profile

Top to bottom: Figs 7, 8 and 9.

rod, placed to more correctly agree with photographs. Fig. 3 shows these modifications done, plus the front and rear halves of the Ascent Stage joined, the joint line doctored and the docking hatch installed. A sink mark in the plastic under the *LM*'s 'chin' was filled with *Squadron White* putty and wet-sanded smooth. A metal strip (an antenna of some kind?) running up the left side of the hatch would be made from strip stock but I decided to do this after adding the thruster quads as there would be a lot of handling involved in bringing them up to speed. Likewise the support strut out to the fuel tank would be added shortly before painting.

The age of the kit was really apparent at this stage. The fit is frankly atrocious. I removed one of the locating pegs which seemed to be forcing a misalignment of the main halves and used superglue all round to lock up the joint. Adzing, filing, filling and sanding took an hour or two to make the joint line acceptable, which is excessive by modern standards, though it mostly disappeared under paint, as intended.

The Ascent Propulsion System is a featureless cylindrical protrusion at the bottom, and if the model was to be displayed separated it would be a definite candidate for replacement, probably with a turned aluminium part, but, as it would be invisible, no effort was made to modify it.

The Reaction Control System 'quads,' the attitude control rockets around the upper stage, were assembled next, and some of the time it seemed as if I was carving new parts from old plastic. Each mount is a two-part assembly and the fit is terrible (Fig. 4, taken earlier). The parts were joined with superglue and their surfaces filed, adzed and sanded, and the many sinkholes doctored with putty. The mounting holes for the rocket bells were cleaned out with a small drill bit. Two rounds of filling were needed, and it was quite obvious there would be plenty more putty involved in mounting them to the hull.

Photographs were studied to find the proper alignment of these mounts (there was a lot of play in the parts and in the case of the rear units almost no definite alignment guide was provided). They were then attached with superglue and the joints doctored with plastic shims and thinned putty, and it was on to another round of sanding back.

The rocket bells themselves were drilled out for realism, painted dark silver with black throats and attached (after main painting) as per the kit instructions. The built-in alignment is wrong, incidentally, but rebuilding the mounts as a whole at this scale is a recipe for a migraine, and I decided to let it lie until I came to fit the parts and see what I could do then. The lower four thrusters have the thrust deflectors moulded integrally, which is incorrect as they were mounted on a system of struts belonging to the Descent Stage.

Final scratchbuilt details for the Ascent Stage were the strut and the 'antenna', and I tackled the latter first. I shaped some .020" strip, cut tiny pieces about 1.5mm long and

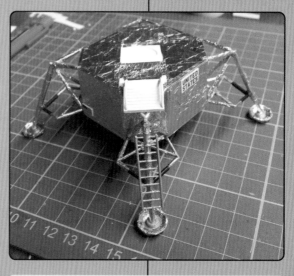

Top to bottom: Figs 10, 11 and 12.

superglued them into place up the side of the hatch and the corresponding fascia of the upper hull as the supports, then laid .010" x .020" *Microstrip* in position over tiny blobs of superglue to hold it in place. The tricky bit is that this strip must bend and run alongside the rendezvous radar antenna housing above the cockpit, and this was a matter of forcing the plastic into contact with supports and holding it until the glue cured.

The strut was added from .060" rod, which was carefully sanded at each end to match the required angles, and superglued into place. Fig. 5 shows these final modifications.

The collection of antennae clustered around the top of the Ascent Stage were delicate, thus they were saved for addition after painting. The six locator holes for them were masked with *Humbrol Maskol* and left to dry.

The first step in getting her through the paint shop was to check the joint work with primer. I masked the windows with tiny pieces of *Tamiya* tape, then mixed a light grey in *Tamiya* acrylics and shot a light coat overall. The main joints had been worked pretty intensively and were in good shape, but a couple of the puttied areas around the thruster mounts needed some extra attention, the strut needed blending in better, and – inevitably when working with so small a subject – some fine details were damaged during the sanding process and needed to be repaired. These were all attended to and an extra coat of primer revealed the beast to be ready for topcoating.

Fig. 6 shows the Ascent Stage reprimed, alongside the foiled Descent Stage (below).

Painting began with a coat of *Tamiya X-11 Silver*. This would become the metal strips which secured the insulation over each facet or panel of the central hull, plus the natural metal of the docking hatch recess. The acrylic dried quickly and the strips were masked with fine-cut pieces of *Tamiya* tape (more of them than I could count – certainly over 120 pieces of tape came off later), which had been further de-glued with a number of pull-offs from my hand. With the network of metallic established I could match the remaining colours to photographs and pick a pattern from the variations seen on different spacecraft. Basically the rest of the ship is either a pale buff-grey or a black/dark grey, and the conventional wisdom is to apply the lighter colour first. However, the arrangement of the panels on sharp edges conspired to make me do it backwards to ease masking. That meant two or three coats of the lighter colour. The 'porch' platform below the hatch would be painted at this time too, in the lighter colour, and mounted to the Descent Stage.

I mixed the dark colour from *XF-1 Flat Black* and *XF-63 German Grey* (1:1). The original may indeed be black, but the lighting conditions vary so widely that it is hard to be sure. Also, lightening the shade a little provides a scale-colour effect. I applied it carefully and let it dry thoroughly before cutting swatches of de-glued tape to mask the black areas of the hull, many of them simply outlined with tape and filled in with *Humbrol Maskol*. This took a while: by this point I felt I had been masking the model for two days… pretty intense on a subject only 60mm wide.

The pale colour was a mix of *Tamiya XF-2 White, XF-57 Buff* and *XF-54 Dark Sea Grey* at a ratio of 8:1:1 and thinned 50%, as seems standard with these paints. I mixed enough for a thorough coating, at least twice over every part of the model, to effectively cover the black. I laid it on until the batch was completely used up, then set the model aside to dry thoroughly before I began the task of unpicking two day's worth of masking followed by touching up as required.

The antennae were cleaned up, their location points unmasked, and the probes and dishes painted (satin white on the front of the dishes and their mounts, grey-black on the backs). The mounts appear to have been protected by a silver foil, and while I glued foil on bright-side-out for the most prominent of them, I painted the rest in silver, gold and white as called out by photo references.

Attaching the thrusters was a simple but repetitive job. The mouth of each bell was drilled out, which began with a pinprick to pilot the hole, before using three drill-sizes to open the throat into a shallow dish. The bells were painted chrome silver, the throats flat black, then these were mounted with a tiny drop of superglue (Fig. 7). Surprisingly, the 3mm bells actually feature the coolant ribs of the real thing. By opening the mounting holes with a small drill in a pin vice I was able to line up the angle of the bells correctly, which I did not expect. The plume shields were sprayed black on their faces and edges and brushed into silver on their backs.

Descent Stage

The *Airfix* kit has a simplified structure on the Descent Stage just to the left (facing, right) of the front/ladder leg, which on early *LM*s was a cylindrical piece of equipment. Later *LM*s did not feature this, so I removed it with knife, files and sandpaper before cementing the body and base of the stage together.

The only painted area on the lower stage would be the DPS and its surrounding structure, which were sprayed dark grey before I began foiling the hull. The top area corresponding to the Ascent Stage receivers I left unfoiled, though the actual location peg holes I foiled over and punched through later.

Microscale Metal Foil Adhesive was always going to be the secret weapon on this project and I was lucky enough to pick some up locally. I gave it a test shot on some sprue with a piece of gold foil (yes, it was Easter egg wrapping!) and found it works nicely on larger areas but is a bit 'indefinite' if trying to wrap small rods, which, of course, is what the legs all are. No matter: the Mylar on the original was a loose fit and made the craft seem bulky – 'all wrapped up,' as it were – so an indefinite fit served the purpose. I had previously considered wrapping everything in tissue soaked in white glue to bulk it out, and hoped the foil glue would work over that (which it probably would not have), but this ended up being unnecessary.

The foiling job was a delicate and fiddly one, with much trimming with scissors and waiting for the glue to dry to a tacky consistency before wrapping the foil on. Each leg required 13 pieces; Fig. 8 shows one leg completed and the components for the other three with their joints pre-painted. The Descent Stage needed around fifty, of various sizes and shapes, Fig. 9 showing this process about half way along. The fit of the crinkly foil was probably snugger than the 'drapey' appearance of the real thing but the small scale tends to forgive the error factor. Indeed, the malleability of the foil is pretty amazing; you can gently burnish it to the surface and it will take on the contours quite readily – for instance, the suggestion of tank detail on the underside was completely foiled without difficulty.

The locator points for all the leg components were found by lightly burnishing the foil, then they were opened with the tip of a sharp blade. The legs were assembled with tiny drops of superglue, and were surprisingly rigid when complete. Fig. 10 shows the process of attaching the legs. They really only line up one way, with very little play, which makes it all the stranger that they don't really meet the ground at the same level. A little finagling would be needed to get the beast to sit square, such as adjusting the fit of two of the

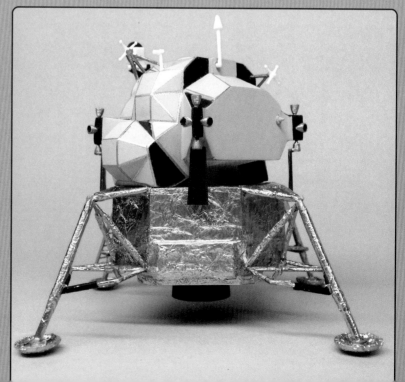

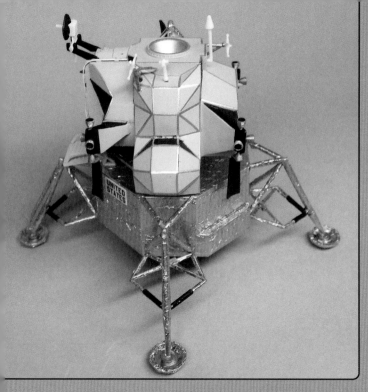

footpads (two legs filed, two legs chocked).

Supergluing the legs into place also resulted in a few slivers of foil going missing, but that was an easy fix, especially as the installation of the parts exposed some bare plastic at the joints which would need patching in any case. Any remaining spots of bare plastic by this point were touched up in gold with a fine brush.

The footpads were also protected with Mylar and experiments showed that wrapping them in foil would be practical as long as the pieces were trimmed to a close size and provided with some cuts around the edge. I painted the central areas gold, then wrapped them and attached them to the legs with liquid glue.

The whole job used less than the wrapping of two smallish Easter eggs: marvellous economy, but in this instance it would have been nice to have had a reason to go out and buy some more!

With the foil in place it was time to apply just two decals from the *Airfix* sheet, 'United States' and a US flag. *Antares* had the words 'United States' stacked vertically and displayed on a white background at the upper middle of the Descent Stage panel to the left of the EVA ladder (right from viewing perspective), while 'Old Glory' was displayed on the opposite panel, low and displaced way to the side. The kit supplies 'United States' on one line, so the decals were trimmed very close and the words separated. I didn't want any surprises with elements of which I had only one, so I overcoated them with *Microscale Liquid Decal Film* to be on the safe side. This was just as well, as the *Airfix* decals were practically useless: first they would not part from the backing film (over ten minutes' soaking, alternately in water or *Micro Set* – by the time 'United' lifted off I was getting ready to use *Microscale* railroad lettering, or create something on custom film instead); then they would not stick to the surface they were applied to: two small placards of .010" styrene (12 x 6mm for the words, 7 x 4mm for the flag) (Fig. 11). I overcoated the decals with *Micro Satin very* carefully, which imparted enough locking factor at the edges to hold them in place. They finally cooperated, but not without more expletives than earned by the last ten models I've built put together. The placards were then glued directly back against the foil (Fig. 12).

I considered building the metal-frame mounts for the thruster plume shields but this would have required punching through the foil in 24 locations to drill mounting holes, and I did not trust myself not to tear the foil in the process, or to accurately mount the struts, which would likely have been of bent wire. Though it is a visible deficiency, I decided to go with *Airfix*'s classic inaccuracy in the name of simplicity.

In the final analysis did I get every detail? Not by a long shot, but, at a scale viewing distance of something like 60 feet, I missed very few of the immediately visible details. Not *too* bad, considering that almost every single component of this kit put up a fight.

The two stages were simply pressed together and the model was complete, making an interesting addition to any Real Space display as it attempts to give an impression of the real craft, in contrast to the often toy-like renditions one sees. I say attempts – it certainly did not receive every possible aspect of the real craft, as, besides being a small model, it is rather a difficult shape to work with. It is also something of an inspiration: I found myself thinking about tripling the dimensions and scratchbuilding it in 1:24th scale, with far more detailed research enabling a really accurate rendition. It's a 'faceted' design; there's nothing that can't be tackled in sheet material, after all. But that's a big job for a future occasion, and for the moment I'm quite pleased with this facelift for an old classic.

References

In addition to a Google Image search, I used photographs from: Bizony, P (2006) *Space: 50 Years of Space Exploration*, Collins, London. Chaikin, A (2002) *Space*, Carlton Books, London. Yenne, W (1985) *The Encyclopaedia of US Spacecraft*, Bison Books, London.

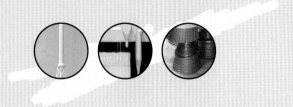

Saturn V three-stage modelling mission—Stage Three:

Building a More Accurate Saturn V

Article and photographs by Alun Owen

Several years ago I was fortunate enough to be on a work trip to Florida and, having a day off, decided to make the trip from the *Orlando Convention Center* out to the Space Coast and the *Kennedy Space Center*. This visit left a lasting impression on me… at the time the shuttle being prepared in the *Vehicle Assembly Building* (which was open as we passed in the bus) was *Columbia*, just prior to its last, fateful mission. The most memorable sight, however, was the utterly monumental *Saturn V*, lying on its side in its purpose-built display hall. Since then I have made a further two trips to Florida, on holiday this time, with each visit including a 'pilgrimage' to the Cape. The most recent, in October 2008 (originally to have included watching the launch of the *Space Shuttle* on *STS-125*, the *Hubble* servicing mission, which finally launched in May 2009), coupled with the 40th Anniversary of the Moon Landing and a group build on the *Science-Fiction and Fantasy Modellers: UK* (*SFM:uk*) website (http://scifimodels.org.uk) gave me the incentive I needed to finally build a model which had been at the back of my mind (and my stock of models) for some time – namely the 1:96 scale *Revell Saturn V*, which I would detail with a resin and photo-etch accurising set from *New Ware Models*.

It is entirely possible to replace virtually every component on the *Revell* kit in the endless pursuit of absolute accuracy, and indeed there are some builds which have accomplished this, but I am not a great scratchbuilder and did not want this build to escalate too dramatically in both cost and time. Also, realistically, I would probably have given up and put it back into the cupboard half finished. I should also add at this stage that I am far from an expert on rocketry and recognise that there are likely to be a number of errors in my build, but it is the overall feel which is perhaps more important (at least to me) than absolute precision, although I *have* attempted to be as accurate as possible.

Model and detailing parts

The 1:96 *Revell* kit – my version is from the previous release for the 25th Anniversary of the Moon Landing – is an impressive thing. The box itself must be over a metre long, and the size of the components (in particular the collars which make up the tubular part of the stack) give some clue as to how big the final model will be. However, it is clear, even with a fairly cursory look, that the parts have been simplified for moulding purposes, and that there are some oddities in the design, which I will cover as we progress. In addition, and common to virtually all kits of the *Saturn V* available, this one is based on (I believe) the *Facilities Integration Vehicle 500-F*, which had some differences from any of the flown *Saturn V*s. Indeed, the fine details changed from vehicle to vehicle as it evolved, so it is necessary to check as many reference photographs plus sources available on the

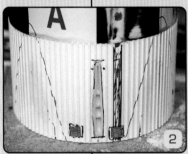

Web as one can to ensure maximum accuracy. My hard drive currently has many, many photographs on it from various sources, including *NASA*'s excellent archives, which were essential references during the build process, although even with these to hand I am sure there are errors and oversights in my build.

The *New Ware* kit provides replacements for a number of *Revell*'s plastic parts, in both resin and photo-etched brass, to correct the details they represent, as well as additional parts for those which are not represented at all on the *Revell* kit. There are, as stated, differences between rockets, so the exact combination and position of parts will depend on what is required for the actual vehicle being built, but I believe everything is supplied to enable any variant to be built. In addition, I ordered a set of replacement decals, plus the *Real Space Models Blast Protection Cover*, which sits over the *Command Module* during launch, and to which the *Escape Tower* is joined.

First Stage (S-1C)

Working from the bottom upwards I kicked off my build with the First Stage (S-1C). This section took me the longest, since at this point I had to get a lot of the fundamentals, including the display system, sorted out. My description of this section also contains the most detail as many of the aspects I describe are equally applicable to the other stages.

What first becomes apparent when you start to build the kit is that, for a variety of reasons (probably cost, size of components, packaging, etc.), *Revell* decided to provide the plain parts of each stage as flat pieces of plastic sheet (commonly called 'the wraps' on a number of other builds, so I will stick with this terminology) which form into tubes and are secured with long pieces of plastic which form the exterior cold helium and electrical umbilical tunnel. The remaining components of each stage are created with circular collars, representing the corrugated sections covered in stringers, which hold the wraps in place. Replacing the wraps with plastic tube (available from *EMA Model Supplies* in a size which is close but requires modification) would have added considerably to the build cost, so I decided to push ahead with the existing parts. With hindsight, and were I ever to do this again, I would bite the bullet and purchase the tubing. *Revell* provide holes in the wraps and pins in the tunnel pieces to help align everything but, on my kit at least, these did not line up properly. Instead I used the collars to provide me with the correct diameter then glued and clamped the wraps together. The resulting stage is surprisingly robust (picture 1, shown with *Revell* umbilical tunnel in place and not the final, modified version).

There are relatively few additional resin parts from the *New Ware* kit on this stage, but of these some are difficult to fit, namely the resin inserts which go around the base. These represent the points at which the *Saturn V* would have been clamped down prior to launch and require holes to be drilled out in the *Revell* parts to accommodate them, the thickness of the plastic making this difficult. The holes which eventually emerged, after considerable drilling and grinding, were not an exact fit and the parts

1. The 'wraps', which form the plain parts of the stage, in place with the moulded, ribbed collars. 2. Resin detail parts are provided in the *New Ware* kit for the hold-downs at the base of the First Stage. 3. Photo-etched parts being added to the First Stage, including the considerably more detailed Cold Helium and Electrical Umbilical Tunnel.

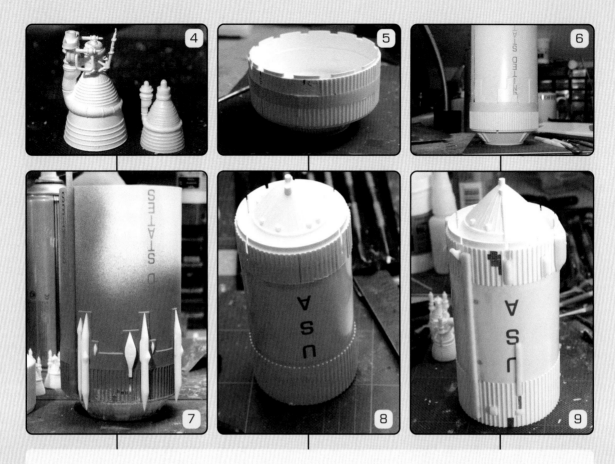

4. The *Revell* F1 engines in comparison with the much plainer, 1:144 *Airfix* version. The size difference is particularly noticeable. 5. Stringers have to be removed from the bottom of the Second Stage. 6. The insulation around the base of the Second Stage can be added with careful measuring from pieces of sheet plastic. 7. Resin and photo-etch parts have been glued in place after carefully consulting the instructions. 8. The simple Third Stage is a nice change as it is much smaller and more manageable than the first two stages. 9. The resin and photo-etch parts added to the Third Stage.

required some filling to get them flush to the surface (picture 2). I mounted them a tiny bit higher than the surrounding plastic and sanded them back. You will also note that the stringers have been removed at these points. This was the case when locating a number of the additional parts, and checking the reference pictures allowed for the correct areas to be removed.

You will notice lots of drawn-on markings I added to the surfaces. I found these really helpful in getting things straight in my own mind as to where everything was to go, and they helped me avoid a few mistakes along the way. This exercise is especially helpful if you build in fits and starts, as I do, as otherwise you may forget where modifications need to be made.

The most obvious additions to S-1C from the *New Ware* kit are the detailing parts which cover the umbilical tunnel. These photo-etched parts wrap over the plastic for the tunnel but the part provided by *Revell* is way too tall. Grinding it down is one option, but I chose instead to replace it totally with lengths of 6.4mm half-round plastic. This worked well and the photo-etched parts are an excellent fit to the half-round strips. The small addition of some strips of plastic along the smooth parts was required to bring them up to the same level as the stringers; this also helping to deal with the overlap which is present on the wraps, as the edge of the tunnel can be positioned to run along the join. The black line in picture 3 represents the centre-line, which is an important reference point in assembling the stack to ensure everything is aligned.

From this point it was possible to begin adding the various connection panels, provided by *New Ware* as photo-etched parts, to the stage, and the level of detail which would eventually be on the kit began to appear (picture 3).

With many of the photo-etched parts in place I felt it was time to turn my attention to what goes underneath the stage and those five mighty F1 engines (picture 4). The level of detail provided in the kit parts is surprisingly high, with a number of parts going to make up each engine and the piping which runs down from the stage above. Clean up is a little tricky, since the engine bells are moulded in two halves, but *is* achievable if you take a little time over it. However, there is a hollow space inside the bell behind the turbine exhaust manifold (the raised part which runs around the engine bell about halfway down) which needs filling if the model is to be displayed on its side as it is at the *Kennedy Space Center*.

Second Stage (S-II)

With the First Stage nearing some level of completion I decided to move onto the Second. The most annoying problem I hit involved the stringers on the bottom of the stage being too long on the original *Revell* parts, which meant grinding off the excess (picture 5). The tape was a good guide and, although very messy, it didn't take too long to remove them all and sand the surfaces flat.

My next move was to install the insulation which sits above the stringers. I did this with a loop of sheet styrene cut to the correct height. Further pieces were then cut, following the plans in the *New Ware* instructions. Helpfully these are shown in 1:192 scale, so everything can be doubled up to get to 1:96. There are five sections of insulation which project up the stage (picture 6).

A coat of grey primer revealed the points where the joins showed, and the addition of some *Mr Dissolved Putty* (a great product for filling seam lines and little areas and well worth hunting down) was added to these and sanded down. The final result was pretty reasonable and didn't take as long as I had feared. One of the most time consuming tasks was ensuring that all the edges had a 45-degree bevel on them. ...Oh, and before anyone comments, I *do* realise that the United States 'decal' is upside down! I glued the collar together without comparing it to the orientation of the first stage and then actually noticed that I had assembled it the other way around – no big deal as it would all be painted over and new decals added anyway.

I was now in a position to add some of the resin parts to the stage. There are quite a few of these around the bottom and, after cutting them from their casting stubs, these were superglued in place (picture 7). Working out their positions is probably the most time consuming thing. In fact, that is pretty much a good description of the whole build, as a lot of time is spent deciphering the instructions, working out which way round to put things together and trying to interpret the frankly appalling *Revell* instructions. The only thing I would add about *New Ware*'s instructions is that often you are left scratching your head as to whether the original *Revell* parts should be included or not.

The top collar was added to the second stage and the section was fairly well complete.

10. The *Revell* interstage with the four ullage thrusters which are seen on most flown *Saturn Vs*. 11. Interstage with original part on the left and replacement on the right. 12. *SLA* with clear window section filled in and painted over. 13. *SLA* with the difficult photo-etch parts added.

14. Original *Revell* moulding shows the *SM* of a Block 1 *Saturn V* rather than the correct Block 2 version of flown *Saturn Vs*. 15. The Block 2 *SM* takes shape with the *New Ware* photo-etch parts. 16. The *Blast Protection Cover* is moulded from vacuformed plastic and covers the *Command Module*.

Third Stage (S-IVB)

I had originally planned to replace the wrap for this section with a new piece of stock sheet, but I didn't have anything of the right thickness, so went with the kit part. The reason for replacing it was that it had been slightly damaged at one end, but it worked out OK with the application of a little filler. Otherwise this stage was pretty simple, being just a collar at each end plus the wrap (picture 8).

There are (for such a small piece) quite a number of resin parts to add, and a number of the stringers needed to be cut short to accommodate these (picture 8). I got a couple of parts wrong – placing them on *top* of the stringers – and, when checking, found that they needed to be cut *into* them. This is the sort of silly error you make when you try and work too quickly and don't check beforehand.

Interstages

I hadn't until now touched any of the interstage parts but they looked like pretty easy components and I thought I would tick them off my list. The interstage between the first and second stages is shown in picture 10. Unfortunately, because *Revell* based their model on the test version this had eight ullage thrusters, whereas flown versions only had four (and later ones none). This meant trimming off every other one of the mounting points that had been moulded in. *New Ware*'s resin thrusters fit nicely onto the stage.

The second of the interstages, between the second and third stages, is also a pretty simple task. This has just four little 'nodules'. There isn't really a lot of difference between the *Revell* ones and the *New Ware* replacements, but as I had them anyway I chose to replace the kit versions. In picture 11 the original is on the left and new one on the right.

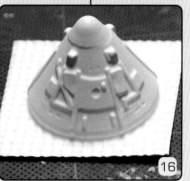

Lunar Module Adapter (SLA)

The first thing that needs to be fixed on the *SLA* is the clear window, provided in the *Revell* kit so you can see the *Lunar Module* inside. This is a relatively easy fix because it can simply be painted over, but it did require a little filler to mount it flush to the surface.

The *SLA* is also quite tricky because there are large and highly bendable pieces of photo-etch to add and these need to be lined up very carefully to form the sections which would have opened up to reveal the *Lunar Exploration Module* (*LEM*). I took my time and tried to fit them as carefully as possible, the final result being reasonable, although there were a couple of points where it was a bit of a battle of wills (picture 13).

The bottom section of this piece is actually the instrument unit (*IU*), which should really be a separate piece. If the model is being built as separate stages this needs to be carefully removed.

Service Module (SM)

Working my way ever upwards I next came to the *Service Module* (*SM*). Unfortunately, pretty much everything here is wrong. The model is based on the *Block 1* version (see picture 14 for the *Revell* version), which never actually flew and which, following the tragedy of *Apollo 1*, was completely redesigned into the *Block 2* version.

All the detail therefore needed to be sanded away and more photo-etch is provided in the *New Ware* kit, which is added to replicate the correct details. This was really

confusing because the plastic retains the appearance of the moulding even after it has been sanded off, so it isn't until you get a coat of primer onto it that you can really tell whether you have a smooth surface or not. The radiator panels were added back from the *New Ware* photo-etch to represent the *Block 2* version (picture 15). The *SM* received a coat of aluminium spray paint at this stage and the radiators were hand painted in white.

Blast Protection Cover (BPC)

The top of the stack is completed with a part which is completely absent from the *Revell* kit – the *Blast Protection Cover* (*BPC*). This covers the *Command Module* (*CM*) and it is to this (and not the *CM* as replicated by *Revell*) that the *Escape Tower* is attached. This is supplied by *Real Space Models* as a vacuformed part (picture 16).

Painting

Now seemed an appropriate time to start masking up the rest of the stack to get a coat of black paint on to form the roll pattern. Masking was done with *Tamiya* tape for the precise edges and something a little cheaper (regular masking tape and paper) for the larger areas (picture 17).

Revell's instructions appear to be wrong at a number of points, or at least don't match either reference or *New Ware*'s instructions. They do, for instance, include a continuous black band around the bottom of *S-IC*, which doesn't seem to be present on the real thing.

Even though I took my time in masking, the ribs make it quite difficult to get a really tight edge, and the resin parts add to this problem. There were a few areas where there was a small amount of leakage underneath and some repainting was needed to get nice, clean edges.

The fins (not mentioned previously as this was an aspect of the build I put off for a while) are the covers supplied from *New Ware* as resin parts. These were masked up so that half were painted black and then the bottoms were sprayed with aluminium (picture 18).

The *SM*, having been primed in white, had its radiator panels masked up while the rest of the module was painted with aluminium (picture 19).

Decals

The *New Ware* kit comes with a set of decals, needed because the *Revell* kit has its markings mainly pre-printed onto the wraps and these are lost during building and painting. The sheet also includes lots of tiny markings

17. The black roll pattern is masked up with tape. Note: The pattern is actually incorrect in this picture as it lacks the complete band of black around the bottom of the Second Stage. 18. The fins masked up for spraying. 19. *SM* masked up to retain the white radiators.

which are barely visible. Although they generally went on well some care is required because they are extremely thin and vulnerable to splitting.

Conclusions

With the decals in place this pretty much wrapped up the build of this stacked model. An alternative idea would be to separate each component and build it on its side [see Gary Welsh's article elsewhere in this volume – Ed.], which would have the added advantage of displaying the detail and interesting areas underneath each stage – the rocket engines of the Second Stage, for example – and detail parts are provided by *New Ware* for this very busy area.

New Ware's parts provide another level of detail to this kit, which I feel is needed for so large a model, although I must acknowledge that, once painted in its monochrome scheme, many of the parts added do have a tendency to disappear, but they *are* there and a closer inspection reveals the detail and keeps you looking at the model.

Of course, the final detailing decals added were those for *Apollo 11* to commemorate the Anniversary of the First Moon Landings.

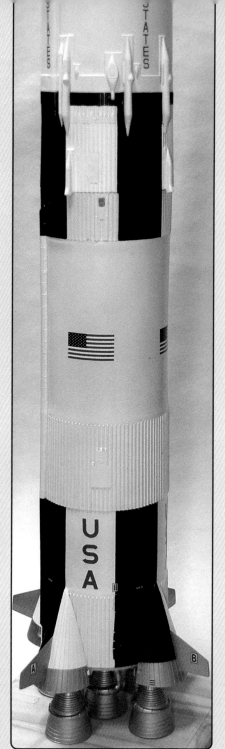

Websites

A blogged diary of this build can be found at: http://alunowen.org
Apollo Maniacs:
http://apollomaniacs.web.infoseek.co.jp/apollo/indexe.htm
John Duncan's Apollo-Saturn Reference Page:
http://www.apollosaturn.com/
NASA Apollo Reference Site:
http://spaceflight.nasa.gov/gallery/images/apollo/index.html
New Ware Models: http://mek.kosmo.cz/newware/
Rick Sternbach's Saturn V Clinic:
http://www.ricksternbach.com/SatV/Saturn_V_Clinic.html
Real Space Models: http://www.realspacemodels.com/